Confucius

Confucius
His Life and Legacy in Art

Lu Wensheng

Julia K. Murray

Edited by J. May Lee Barrett

China Institute Gallery
China Institute
New York
2010

Distributed by Art Media Resources, Ltd

The catalogue was published to accompany the exhibition
Confucius: His Life and Legacy in Art, organized by the
China Institute Gallery in collaboration with the
Shandong Provincial Museum

Presented at

China Institute Gallery
125 East 65th Street
New York, NY 10065
212.744.8181
February 11–June 13, 2010

© 2010 China Institute in America. All rights reserved.
Library of Congress Control Number: 2009936918
ISBN-10: 0-9774054-5-1
ISBN-13: 978-0-9774054-5-9

General Editor and Project Director: Willow Weilan Hai Chang
Consulting Editor: J. May Lee Barrett
Chinese Editor: Zhou Xiaolu
Translations: David Huiwei Shen
                 Zou Xin
Catalogue Designer: Peter Lukic
Exhibition Designer: Perry Hu
Photos courtesy of Shandong Provincial Museum,
    unless otherwise indicated
Printed in the United States of America

Note to the Reader
Chinese is romanized in the *pinyin* system throughout the text
and bibliography except for the names of Chinese authors writing
in Western languages. Chinese terms cited in Western-language
titles remain in their original form and have not been converted.

Cover illustration (detail, cat. no. 1): Anonymous. *Portrait of
Confucius as Minister of Justice in Lu.* Shandong Provincial Museum

Frontispiece (detail, cat. no. 4): *Confucius hears the Shao music in
the state of Qi,* in *Traces of the Sage (Pictorial Biography of Confucius).*
The Confucius Museum in Qufu, Shandong Province

Back cover (imprint of cat. no. 35): "Imperially bestowed 'Poetry,
Documents, Ritual, Music'" seal. The Confucius Museum in Qufu,
Shandong Province

SPONSORS OF THE EXHIBITION — vi

MESSAGE FROM THE BOARD AND PRESIDENT — viii
Virginia A. Kamsky, Sara Judge McCalpin

MESSAGE FROM THE SHANDONG PROVINCIAL MUSEUM — ix
Lu Wensheng

FOREWORD — x
Willow Weilan Hai Chang

ACKNOWLEDGEMENTS — xiii
Julia K. Murray

CHRONOLOGY — xiv

TIMELINE OF CONFUCIUS'S LIFE — xv

MAPS — xvi

ESSAYS
Confucius, His Philosophy and Cultural Relics — 1
Lu Wensheng
More than One Confucius at a Time: Teacher, Statesman, God — 13
Julia K. Murray

CATALOGUE — 30

BIBLIOGRAPHY — 107

CHINA INSTITUTE GALLERY EXHIBITIONS: 1966–2009 — 113

Sponsors of the Exhibition

*This exhibition, exhibition-related programming, and catalogue
have been made possible in part through the generous support of the following ***

BENEFACTOR

National Endowment for the Arts

PATRON

E. Rhodes and Leona B. Carpenter Foundation
New York State Council on the Arts
Mary Lawrence Porter

CONTRIBUTORS

New York City Department of Cultural Affairs
Anla Cheng and Mark Kingdon
Carolyn Hsu-Balcer and René Balcer
Amie and Tony James
Miranda Wong Tang

Message from the Board and President

The philosophy of Confucianism has pervaded Chinese culture for centuries, and thus, it has been a significant area of study for scholars and students. China Institute is proud to present *Confucius: His Life and Legacy in Art*, one of the first major exhibitions in the U.S. to explore the significance of his cultural influence by tracing the ways he has been imagined and venerated over the centuries. This exhibition introduces many unfamiliar and intriguing aspects of Confucius and his descendants through an array of material and visual culture. The various extant and excavated artifacts from Shandong, the birthplace of Confucius, dating from the Shang to Qing Dynasties, bring to life the complex legacy of Confucius's ideologies and recall the magnitude of Chinese history and civilization.

Confucius once said, "I am not one who knew about things at birth; I am one who through my admiration of antiquity is keen to discover things" (*The Analects*, 7.20). Of the ancient Chinese philosopher's profound and timeless adages, this one succinctly describes the motivation that drives many of China Institute Gallery's ambitious exhibitions. China Institute is very fortunate to collaborate with the Shandong Provincial Museum and the Confucius Museum in Qufu on this important and ground-breaking exhibition and catalogue. We are grateful to them for working with us to bring these significant artworks to America and to illustrate the life and legacy of one of China's most influential icons.

In 2005, shortly after the establishment of the Confucius Institute at China Institute, the idea to have an exhibition on Confucius was conceived and discussed at a senior staff meeting. *Confucius: His Life and Legacy in Art* represents a new initiative to take full advantage of our unique exhibitions by expanding our Institute-wide programming and online resources. Our thanks are extended to Willow Hai Chang, Director of China Institute Gallery, who has led this project from its development to its completion. We are grateful to the guest curators and authors of the catalogue, Mr. Lu Wensheng, Director of the Shandong Provincial Museum, and Professor Julia K. Murray of the University of Wisconsin, Madison who are eminent scholars of Confucian art history and culture. Their research presented in this publication is a result of a deep commitment to expanding the scholarship on Confucian culture. We extend our gratitude to all the Gallery staff and the participants in this project because it would not have materialized without their dedication and diligent work.

Chinese art has long served as an ambassador of Chinese culture and history to the American people, and China Institute is proud to take part in this engaging and effective cultural exchange. We extend our sincere gratitude to the Administration of Cultural Relics of Shandong Province for their endorsement of the project and entrusting these artworks to China Institute for the exhibition. We could not succeed in fulfilling our mission without the continuing support of our Trustees, our Gallery Committee, the Sponsors of the Exhibition, and, of course, our loyal Friends of the Gallery, to all of whom we are especially grateful.

Virginia A. Kamsky
Chair, Board of Trustees

Sara Judge McCalpin
President
China Institute in America

Message from the Shandong Provincial Museum

About 2500 years ago, the great thinker and educator Confucius was born in Qufu, in the ancient state of Lu. This was the most culturally developed place in China at that time. Living on this piece of culturally fertile earth, Confucius had in his youth become determined to study. His saying, "Traveling in a group of three, there must be a teacher for me" (among three people, one of them is certainly good enough to be a teacher) summarizes his advice about learning from others. After reaching maturity, Confucius devoted himself to politics and traveled to many states. In his later years, he lectured to an audience of disciples, thus founding Confucianism (*ruxue*). In the course of its enrichment by successive generations of scholars, Confucianism gradually became the orthodox and mainstream ideology of ancient China. Confucius and his beliefs dominated Chinese history, influenced East Asia, and to this day continue to influence China and the rest of the world.

Today, two thousand years since the inception of Confucian ideology, why do the ideas of Confucius still possess formidable vitality in a society that has entered the information age? The reason is that Confucianism advocates "benevolence," or the idea that "the benevolent man loves humanity." It advocates "propriety," as in a society where the individual "subdues the self and observes propriety," thereby complying with the social order. Confucianism advocates the "doctrine of the mean," which advises people not to go to extremes in handling ones affairs. People should resolve their conflicts in a conciliatory manner. Confucianism also advocates "harmony," particularly "existing in harmony while maintaining differences" and social harmony. It promotes "education for everyone without distinction of class." These ideas should be the universal truths of human society. Therefore, Confucius and the vitality of Confucian thought is still strong today.

It is our hope that you will be inspired when viewing this exhibition of precious relics related to Confucius and Confucianism that we have brought from his birthplace and that it will enhance your understanding of Confucian thought. I want to thank the China Institute for its contributions to cultural exchange between China and the United States throughout its nearly hundred-year history. Cultural exchange is the communication of the human spirit; it is the sincerest communication.

Lu Wensheng
Director
Exhibition co-curator

Foreword

There was an exceptional time in the history of mankind, an intellectually exciting period, in which so many of the world's great philosophers in the West and in the East thrived. The great names of that period, from the sixth through fourth centuries BCE, resonate to this day; they include, for instance, Socrates, Plato, Aristotle, Gautama Buddha, Laozi, and Confucius.

In China, Confucius (551–479 BCE) promoted an ideal—a harmonious society grounded upon the rites and institutions originated by the Duke of Zhou (ca. 1100 BCE). Although this dream was not achieved in Confucius's lifetime, three hundred years later the Han dynasty emperor Wudi (157–87 BCE) accepted a suggestion by the scholar and political theorist Dong Zhongshu (179–104 BCE) to respect Confucian ideology above all others. Since then, Confucian thought contributed greatly to Chinese society as the ideological foundation of China's long-lasting feudal dynasties and an ethical guide for human interaction in everyday life. Thus, the term "Confucius says," became very popular in verbal and written discourse. Nevertheless, opposition to his influence occurred during different historical periods, notably the criticism during the 1919 May Fourth Movement that Confucianism suppressed freedom and individuality. It is unclear whether that result was something Confucius wanted or whether it was a contrivance of those who used and twisted his ideology based on their own understanding and needs. However, his genuine belief in benevolence, justice, ritual, loyalty, and filial piety as the basic qualities of all human beings has timeless value for the building of an ideal harmonious world.

The Western world first heard of Confucius some four hundred years ago in the late sixteenth century. Through missionaries and more direct trade with China, Europeans gradually came to know China not only as the rich and beautiful country Marco Polo had described centuries earlier, but also as a great country possessing deep wisdom. Confucius was studied and warmly praised by many intellectuals in the West, such as Sir William Temple (1628–1699) and Voltaire (1694–1778). However, general ignorance of "oriental" culture in the U.S. began to wane just less than a century ago, when the great literary works of China were being translated and popularized by such Western scholars as Witter Bynner and Arthur Waley and the foundations of the great museum collections of Asian art were being laid.

Outside China, Confucius has been highly regarded by its neighboring countries for more than a thousand years, and he has become an icon of the deep wisdom to be found in traditional oriental culture. That he should receive a warm response and support in the increasingly materialistic and industrialized setting of today's world, however, is somewhat remarkable. His words were recited at the magnificent opening ceremony of the Beijing Olympics in August 2008, and, moreover, a grand sacrificial ceremony is conducted every year on his birthday (September 28) at his hometown in Qufu, Shandong, as well as in other communities around Asia. On October 28, 2009, the U.S. House of Representatives voted overwhelmingly to honor the 2,560th anniversary of Confucius's birth, a gesture of respect for Chinese culture. Thus, the significance of this exhibition has already exceeded our expectations. It is our hope that in these works of art, the viewer will "see" Confucius and realize his continuing relevance. The world needs justice and wisdom, the world needs benevolence, and the world still needs Confucius. His ideal world can be a dream for all of us.

We are indeed proud to present this first-of-its-kind art exhibition in the United States. The seed was sown in 2004 while I was working on the exhibition "Providing for the Afterlife: 'Brilliant Artifacts' from Shandong." During a conversation with Xie Zhixiu, deputy director of the Shandong Provincial Cultural Bureau, he suggested with a confident tone that, in Shandong, "we have more things to share with the world. *We* have Confucius, and it could be another exhibition." My reaction was that everyone knows Confucius as a philosopher, so how can that be reflected through artwork? At that time, I could only think of the various *Kongzi shengji tu* (Pictures of the traces of the sage Confucius). Therefore, I just smiled politely without saying anything. Fortuitously, the China Institute was named in 2005 by the Office of Chinese Language Council International, or Hanban, to be the first location of their Confucius Institute in New York City. At one of our weekly senior staff meetings, I mentioned that a Confucius exhibition would now be very relevant and offered great potential for related programs. Although the idea was well received, I still had to find out how many works of art would support this theme. I went to Shandong again, and during the course of viewing exhibitions there and digging around museum storerooms, the structure and concept of this exhibition took shape. The artwork would be selected and arranged according to the following three themes: his life, his teachings, and his later veneration. We were to once again have the special pleasure of collaborating with the Shandong Provincial Museum on an exhibition.

This project would not have been possible without the cooperation and support of various officials and cultural institutions in China. My particular thanks go to Xie Zhixiu for his initial suggestion and continued support; to Lu Wensheng, director of the Shandong Provincial Museum, for his gentlemanly response to our needs; to Zhao Jiqun, the former director of the Confucius Museum in Qufu, for several enjoyable meetings to discuss this exhibition and for his answers to unresolved questions at the very last minute; to Kong Xiangsheng, the current director of the

Confucius Museum, for picking up the project and seeing it through to the finish; and especially to Jiang Qun, curator of the Shandong Provincial Museum's Collection Department, for her patience and persistence in dealing with the thousands of details necessary to ensure that pieces of the logistic puzzle come together. I also would like to take this opportunity to thank all the staff in the Shandong Provincial Museum and Confucius Museum for their patient assistance.

Back in the U.S., my heartfelt gratitude is extended to all the sponsors of this exhibition and those in the China Institute community who have remained our dedicated supporters. I feel especially honored to receive funding from the National Endowment for the Arts, New York State Council on the Arts, and the New York City Department of Cultural Affairs. The commitment of our loyal Friends of the Gallery continues to energize us to always pursue being the best. Our Board of Trustees, led by Virginia Kamsky, and our Gallery Committee, led by Diane Schafer, have been an unending source of encouragement. I am also indebted to the Gallery Committee for supporting this special kind of art exhibition and suggesting that we invite Julia K. Murray, Professor of Art History, East Asian Studies and Religious Studies at the University of Wisconsin at Madison, to join Lu Wensheng as a guest co-curator; together they shared the work of researching and interpreting the individual objects. The multi-perspective introductions by these two scholars combine to add a profound weight to the project.

I am grateful for the help of various scholars and professionals in bringing this publication to press. J. May Lee Barrett made invaluable recommendations and brought her academic background in Asian art history and experience with book production to her role as editor. Professor Zhou Xiaolu responded to our urgent request for help in editing and revising the Chinese text, and

Mr. Liu Boqin assisted in the research. The challenging work of translating was for the most part carried out by David Huiwei Shen with additional contributions by Zou Xin and others. Finally, the handsome design of this book and its maps is the work of Peter Lukic. In addition, the beautiful installation of the exhibition is the result of the creative design and labor of Perry Hu. Nicole Straus and Margery Newman's efforts brought this show to the public's attention.

My dedicated gallery staff, Sara Tam, Mia Park, and Yue Ma, worked tirelessly and diligently on the numerous tasks involved in this project and saw to their successful completion. My thanks also go to Donna Thomas and her staff in the Development Department for their assistance in raising funds and organizing related events and to the Education Department for producing the valuable programs that will maximize the significance of the exhibition for the public. A special note of appreciation goes to Sara Judge McCalpin, President of China Institute, for her understanding and continued encouragement. She had accompanied me to the Shandong Provincial Museum and the Confucius Museum in the spring of 2007, where we shared the uplifting experience of examining artworks in the storerooms. We also participated in an official ceremony organized by the Qufu city government to bestow a life-size Confucius portrait on the China Institute. These shall be among my most cherished memories.

Willow Weilan Hai Chang
Director
China Institute Gallery

Acknowledgements

I wish to express my profound gratitude to Director Willow Weilan Hai Chang of China Institute Gallery for inviting me to curate this exhibition on Confucius, affording me the precious opportunity to work with objects from important collections in his ancient homeland. It has been a pleasure to collaborate with Director Lu Wensheng of the Shandong Provincial Museum, who generously shared his deep knowledge and passion for China's cultural heritage and warmly extended his hospitality on my visits to Ji'nan. I also thank Director Kong Xiangsheng of The Confucius Museum for making my trips to Qufu productive and enjoyable. The efficient and collegial staff at all three institutions ensured that every phase of preparation went smoothly.

I owe heartfelt thanks to libraries in China and the United States that enabled me to examine rubbings and rare books bearing on works in the exhibition. The Harvard-Yenching Library was a godsend. Also invaluable were the National Library in Beijing, Nanjing Library, and libraries of the University of Chicago and University of Wisconsin.

As an art historian studying images of Confucius, I have learned much from colleagues in Chinese history, literature, and religion. Over the years I have benefited immensely from discussions with Thomas Wilson and his scholarship on state and family cults of Confucius. Conversations and exchanges with Sébastian Billioud, Mark Csikszentmihalyi, P. J. Ivanhoe, Lionel Jensen, Michael Nylan, Deborah Sommer, Jeffrey Wasserstrom, and Tu Wei-ming furthered my understanding of Confucius and his legacy. David Bordwell, Jonathan Chaves, Nicole Huang, and William Nienhauser pointed me toward little-known visual materials that I otherwise would not have found. Among art historians, Robert Bagley, Robert Harrist, Annette Juliano, and Oliver Moore provided much-appreciated encouragement.

I have been fortunate to enjoy generous support for my research on this exhibition. My initial efforts to develop the concept and object list took place during my sabbatical year as a Visiting Scholar at Harvard, with a fellowship jointly funded by the ACLS, SSRC, and NEH. Grants from the Metropolitan Center for Far Eastern Art Studies and University of Wisconsin Graduate School enabled me to travel to Shandong and supported later stages of research and writing. Seminars at the University of Wisconsin in 2007 and 2008 provided opportunities for extended consideration of issues related to Confucius and the visual arts.

Interest in Confucius has grown enormously from the time I began to research images of him, some two decades ago. The topic then seemed idiosyncratic, far from the mainstream not only of art history but of Chinese studies generally. Now, however, Confucius has become not only relevant but arguably even central to contemporary Chinese culture, as ideas associated with him have returned to favor. Large statues of him appear all over China, and best-selling books popularize his teachings, as do cartoons, television series, and movies. It is my hope that this exhibition will place these recent developments in larger context by suggesting the many roles Confucius has played in the past.

Julia K. Murray
University of Wisconsin-Madison
Exhibition co-curator

Chronology of Chinese Dynasties and Historical Periods

XIA DYNASTY (unconfirmed) 夏   ca. 2100– ca. 1600 BCE

SHANG DYNASTY 商   ca. 1600–ca. 1050 BCE

ZHOU DYNASTY 周   ca. 1050–256 BCE

    Western Zhou 西周 (ca. 1050–771 BCE)

    Eastern Zhou 东周 (771–256 BCE)

     Spring and Autumn period 春秋时 (770–ca. 475 BCE)†

     Warring States period 战国时代 (ca. 475–221 BCE)††

QIN DYNASTY 秦   21–206 BCE

HAN DYNASTY 汉   206 BCE –220 CE

    Western Han 西汉 (206 BCE–8 CE)

    Xin 新王莽 (Wang Mang interregnum, 9–23 CE)

    Eastern Han 东汉 (25–220 CE)

THREE KINGDOMS   三国时代

    Wei 魏   220–265

    Shu Han 蜀漢   221–263

    Wu 吳   222–263

JIN DYNASTY 晋   265–420

    Western Jin 西晋 (265–317)

    Eastern Jin 东晋 (317–420)

SOUTHERN AND NORTHERN DYNASTIES 南北朝 (420–589)

Northern Dynasties 北朝

    Northern Wei 北魏   386–534

    Eastern Wei 东魏   534–550

    Northern Qi 北齐   550–577

    Western Wei 西魏   535–556

    Northern Zhou 北周   557–581

Southern Dynasties 南朝

    Liu Song 刘宋   420–479

    Southern Qi 南齐   479–502

    Liang 梁   502–557

    Chen 陳   557–589

SUI DYNASTY 隋   581–618

TANG DYNASTY 唐   618–907

FIVE DYNASTIES 五代 (907–960)

LIAO DYNASTY 辽   907–1125

SONG DYNASTY 宋   960–1279

    Northern Song 南宋 (960–1127)

    Southern Song 北宋 (1127–1279)

JIN DYNASTY 金   1115–1234

YUAN DYNASTY 元   1279–1368

MING DYNASTY 明   1368–1644

QING DYNASTY 清   1644–1911

Prominent states of the
Spring and Autumn period
    Chu 楚 (11th c.–223 BCE)
    Jin 晋 (11th c.–349 BCE)
    Lu 鲁 (10th c.–256 BCE)
    Qi 齐 (11th c.–221 BCE)
    Qin 秦 (9th c.–221 BCE)
    Song 宋 (ca. 1050–286 BCE)
    Wei 卫 (11th c.–209 BCE)
    Wu 吳 (11th c.–473 BCE)
    Yan 燕 (11th c.–222 BCE)
    Yue 越 (?–334 BCE)
    Zheng 郑 (806–375 BCE)

Minor states included in Confucius's travels:
    Cai 蔡 (ca. 1050–447 BCE)
    Cao 曹 (11th c.–487 BCE)
    Chen 陳 (11th c.–479 BCE)

Major powers of the Warring States period
    Qi 齐 (11th c.–221 BCE)
    Chu 楚 (11th c.–223 BCE)
    Yan 燕 (11th c.–222 BCE)
    Han 韩 (403–230 BCE)
    Zhao 赵 (403–222 BCE)
    Wei 魏 (403–225 BCE)
    Qin 秦 (9th c.–221 BCE)

† This period takes its name from the chronicles of the state of Lu, the *Chunqiu* 春秋, or *Spring and Autumn Annals*, which covers the years 722 to 481 BCE.

†† This period is so named after the *Zhanguo ce* 战国策, or *Strategies of the Warring States*, a compilation of texts spanning the years 403 to 221 BCE.

Timetable of Confucius's Life*

551 BCE   Birth of Confucius at Mount Ni, located southeast of Qufu in Lu state
(in present-day Shandong province), traditionally accepted as on September 28.

549 BCE   At the age of three, Confucius's father died.

537 BCE   He was to later say, "I had decided to devote myself to studies and learning
at the age of fifteen."

535 BCE   Around this time, Confucius's mother died. He was 16[†] or 17. Other sources
give this date as 527 BC, when he was 23 or 24.[†]

533 BCE   At the age of 19 he married a woman from the Qiguan family of the Song state.
Around this time, he gained employment as manager of the state granary.

532 BCE   Birth of Confucius's son, who is named Li (Carp), also known as Boyu (Prime Fish),
after Duke Zhao of Lu sent a carp as a gift. Around this time Confucius was promoted
to state husbandry manager.

523 BCE   At 29, Confucius learned to play the *qin* from the famous Master Xiang.

522 BCE   Around this time Confucius started a private school and began to teach.
Later he was to say of himself, "By thirty, one gets established."

518 BCE   Confucius accepts Meng Yizi and Nangong Jingshu as disciples. Jingshu arranges
for Confucius to travel to Luoyang, the Zhou capital, where he meets Laozi.

517 BCE   After a conflict breaks out in Lu state, Confucius, at the age of 34[†] or 35,
is forced to relocate briefly to Qi state.

516 BCE   Confucius returns to Lu.

512 BCE   Later Confucius was to say of himself, "I had no doubts at forty."

501 BCE   At 51, Confucius became the chief magistrate of Zhongdu,
present-day Wenshang county in Shandong Province.

500 BCE   Confucius becomes minister of justice and distinguishes himself at the conference
between Lu and Qi at Jiagu.

497 BCE   At about the age of 54,[†] Confucius headed east to Wei state,
beginning his sojourns in several states to promote his ideology.

494 BCE   In the first year of Duke Ai of Lu, Confucius traveled to Chen state.
He was about 57 years old.[†]

484 BCE   Confucius, at around the age of 68, returned to his hometown, Qufu,
in Lu state and focused on teaching and studying the *Rites of Zhou* (*Zhouli*).

479 BCE   Death of Confucius at the age of 72[†] or 73.

* The story of Confucius's life is drawn from various literary sources, some of which are apocryphal,
whose dates do not always agree. For the purpose of this publication, his birth year is accepted as 551 BCE.
The reader should be aware that in some cases Confucius's stated age is derived from traditional literature
and follows the Chinese custom, which is to begin counting with "one" from birth and increase at the Lunar
New Year rather than the anniversary of the birth. Thus, there is generally a discrepancy of one year.

† By Western count.

Major States of the Spring and Autumn Period and Confucius's Travel Routes

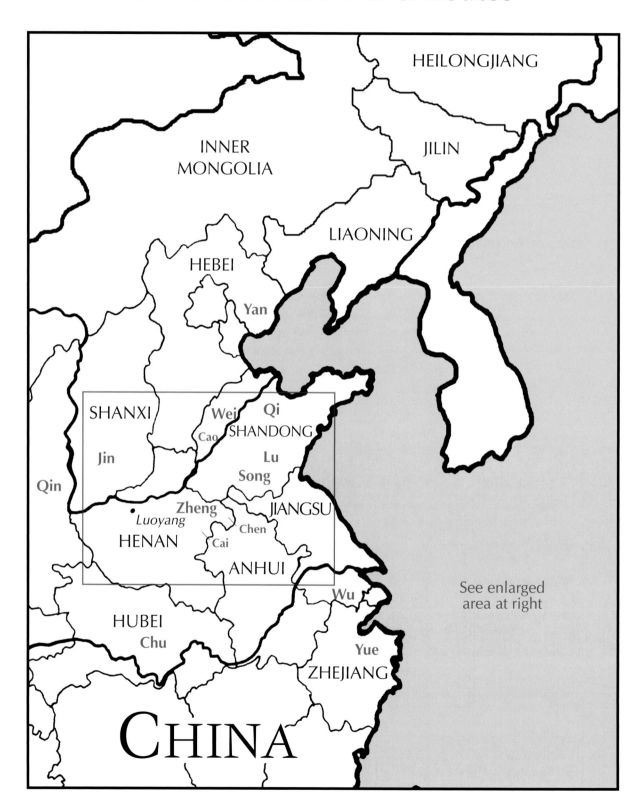

HEILONGJIANG

INNER
MONGOLIA

JILIN

LIAONING

HEBEI

Yan

SHANXI

Wei

Qi

SHANDONG

Cao

Jin

Lu

Song

Qin

Zheng

JIANGSU

Luoyang

Chen

HENAN

Cai

ANHUI

Wu

See enlarged
area at right

HUBEI

Chu

Yue

ZHEJIANG

CHINA

In the thirteenth year of Duke Ding of Lu (497 BCE), when Confucius was 54, he embarked on a journey that took him to many different states. Starting from Lu, he traveled to Wei, Cao, Song, Zheng, Chen, Cai, and possibly Chu. Confucius remained abroad until the eleventh year of Duke Ai of Lu (484 BCE), when at the age of 67 or 68 he returned to the state of Lu. The range of his travels remained mainly within the areas of present-day Shandong and Henan provinces.

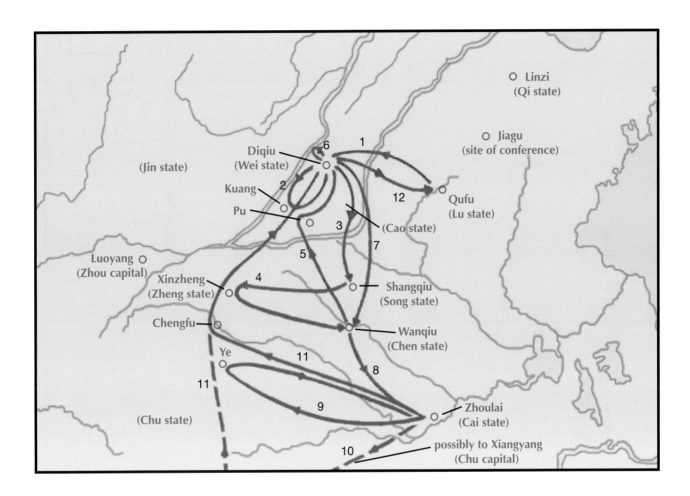

Travel routes

1. Confucius leaves Lu in 497 BCE and stays in Wei 10 months
2. Sets off for Chen, but attacked at Kuang and returns to Wei
3. Once again leaves Wei for Chen, passes through Cao and is attacked at Song
4. Diverted to Zheng for short stay, then arrives in Chen
5. In 494 BCE, decides to return to Wei, but along the way he is briefly held prisoner at Pu
6. Leaves Wei for the Jin state, but after reaching the river turns back to Wei
7. He returns to Chen in 491 BCE
8. In 490 BCE he travels to Cai, a small dependency of the Chu state, and remains through 489 BCE
9. He travels to Ye, another Chu district, after a short stay he returns to Cai
10. According to Sima Qian in the *Shiji*, "Kongzi shijia," Confucius is invited to visit the king of Chu
11. Returns to Wei, where he would remain about 5 years
12. Returns to Lu in 484 BCE

Principal structures of the Confucius Temple

1. The Ten-Thousand-Fathom Wall (Wanren gongqiang)
2. Gate of Golden Sound and Stirring Jade
   (Jinsheng yuzhen)
3. Pan Pond Bridge (Panshuiqiao)
4. Lattice Star Gate (Lingxingmen)
5. Original Ether of Supreme Harmony Archway
   (Taihe yuanqi fang)
6. Ultimate Sage Temple Archway (Zhishengmiao fang)
7. Timeliness of the Sage Gate (Shengshimen)
8. Bi River Bridge (Bishuiqiao)
9. Expanding the Way Gate (Hongdaomen)
10. Gate of the Great Mean (Dazhongmen)
11. Assimilating Culture Gate (Tongwenmen)
12. Star of Literature Pavilion (Kuiwen'ge)
13. Gate of Great Achievement (Dachengmen)
14. Apricot Platform or Terrace (Xingtan)
15. Hall of Great Achievement (Dachengdian)
16. Resting Hall (Qidian)
17. Hall of the Traces of the Sage (Shengjidian)
18. & 19. Thirteen Imperial Stele Pavilions (Shisan beiting)

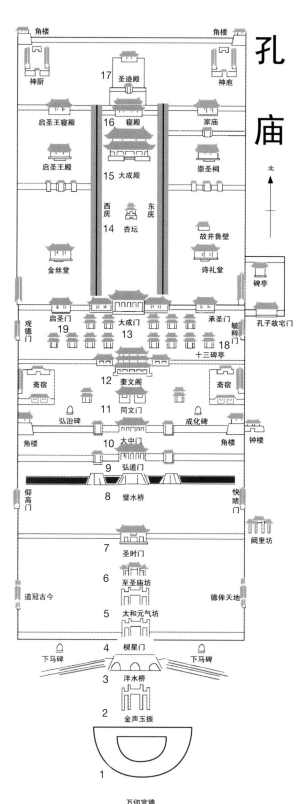

Courtesy of The Confucius Museum in Qufu

Confucius, His Philosophy and Cultural Relics
Lu Wensheng

The great thinker and educator Confucius (Kongzi) was born in 551 BCE in the capital of the Lu state, Qufu, in present-day Shandong province. He was the founder of Confucianism. In 134 BCE, Han dynasty Emperor Wu accepted a proposal to "do away with the hundred schools of thought and honor only Confucianism." This he did, canonizing Confucian philosophy as the governing doctrine of statehood for rulers of succeeding dynasties and subsequent ages. In the more than two millennia since then, the philosophy of Confucius has remained in the mainstream of Chinese thinking and has come to be recognized as a major factor in the continuity of Chinese civilization. Although Confucius left us long ago, the influence of his philosophy is still significant in modern society. At the core of his beliefs were a code of ethics and a moral sense through which proper relationships between individuals could be maintained, a country governed, and social development fostered. Such a vision of ruling through virtue continues to have its affect on modern society, and the guidelines for personal perfection that he proposed are still applicable to the social conduct of modern man.

THE ERA OF GREAT PHILOSOPHERS

Confucius lived in an era known as the Spring and Autumn and Warring States periods (770–221 BCE). It was a time of turbulent change. Not only was Chinese society experiencing great political and economic chaos, but also incredible ideological and cultural activity.

The Spring and Autumn and Warring States periods covered the second half of the long feudal rule of the Zhou dynasty (ca. 1050–256 BCE). Since the founding of the Zhou kingdom, its rulers had been granting "fiefdoms" to its hereditary nobles. The realm was sliced into many "vassal states," whose appointed leaders, known as "hereditary noble dukes," were either family members in the Zhou aristocracy or ministers of merit. These vassal states had their own capitals, political institutions, and

armies, and succession to power was hereditary. The dukes acknowledged allegiance to the king of Zhou, to whom they paid tribute and had obligations to fulfill. As the vassal states became increasingly powerful, the kingdom became fragmented. Although the vassal dukes and princes still acknowledged the legitimacy of the king of Zhou, they showed no subordination to his orders. Because of their individual vested interests, frequent conflicts broke out between the Zhou king and the vassal states and among the vassal states themselves. Powerful vassal states often bullied weaker ones, constantly triggering large-scale wars. At the same time, in order to survive and promote development, a series of political and economic reforms took place within the vassal states. People's ways of thinking were gradually freed from the strict ritual formalities of old institutions. Thus, Confucius lived in an era of political upheaval as well as an era of reconstruction in a new social order.

In this epoch of turbulence and change, a new social class known as the "intelligentsia," or scholar gentry (shi), emerged and became gradually accepted by society. Members of the intelligentsia did not own land, nor did they usually engage in social production. They were, however, highly educated, knowledgeable, and skilled. Specially attached to the service of dukes and princes, nobles, and high officials, they used their knowledge and skills to influence powerful figures of society, and many of them became advisors and assistants to the dukes and officials. The scholars were also active thinkers, avid learners, great socializers, and travelers. Their emergence and growth in ranks accelerated ideological and cultural changes in society, providing the background from which Confucian philosophy emerged and developed.

The Spring and Autumn and Warring States periods constitute the first era of ideological and cultural florescence in Chinese history. In this era of change, a person enjoyed freedom of intellectual thinking, and all kinds of philosophies and schools of thought were born, creating a situation in which, it is described, "a hundred schools contend." The "hundred schools" refer to the various schools of philosophy and branches of thinking, and the "various *zi*" were the masters representing these schools. Most famous among them were Confucianism, established by Kongzi; Daoism (Taoism), established by Laozi; Moism, established by Mozi; and the School of Military Tactics, spearheaded by Sunzi. There were a number of other influential schools, including the School of Law (Legalism), the School of Names (Logicians), the School of Agriculture, and the School of Prosecution. Each of these schools of thought and their masters formulated their own theories and had their unique characteristics. They exchanged arguments and adopted points and ideas from one another. But, in general, the objective of each was to explain and interpret social reality and history, explore the future, and investigate human life and the universe.

It was during the Spring and Autumn and Warring States periods that China's Great Sage, Confucius, was born. At almost the same time, Greek civilization in Europe and Buddhism in ancient India rose and advanced. Greek civilization is the source of European culture; its ancient literature and philosophy once served as benchmarks for Europe's Renaissance. During its course, Greek civilization produced a group of great thinkers, including the likes of Socrates, Plato, and Aristotle. In ancient India, concepts of Buddhism were formulated by Siddhartha Gautama, who came to be venerated by disciples the world over as "the Buddha Himself." Buddhism soon spread all over South Asia, Central Asia, and East Asia. Today, it is one of the three major religions of the world. Thus, the time around Confucius's birth was a world-wide era of scintillating ideological and cultural activity. It was also the beginning of an age of maturity for the world's major cultures and ideologies. Today, China's Confucian thought, Europe's Greek civilization, and ancient India's Buddhism still influence peoples and societies around the world.

THE LIFE OF CONFUCIUS

Confucius's ancestors were members of the aristocracy in the old Song state. When his sixth-generation ancestor Kong Fujia was murdered in a power struggle within the court, his fifth-generation ancestor Mu Jinfu fled to safety in Qufu. Confucius's father, Shuliang He, was a minor military official known among the hereditary noble dukes for his bravery and strength. Confucius's mother was Yan Zhengzai, the third wife of Shuliang He. She married him when she was about twenty years of age and he was sixty-six. Soon after the marriage, she gave birth to Confucius. Because the birth took place at Mount Ni outside the city of Qufu, the child was named Kong Qiu [lit., "small hill"].

Confucius spent his childhood in hardship and misery. His father died when he was three, and his mother left Mount Ni with the young Confucius, relocating to the Queli neighborhood inside Qufu. The hardships of life for a widow and orphan eventually caught up with her, and she died in her thirties, when Confucius was around sixteen or seventeen. Although life was hard, under the teachings of his mother Confucius came to have great ambitions as a child. Confucius once said, "I had decided to devote myself to studies and learning at the age of fifteen." Thus, in his youth he set up the great goal of lifelong learning. Confucius's success had a lot to do with the way his mother educated him and his own childhood aspirations.

Before he gained recognition, Confucius worked at several jobs to provide for the family and had suffered a cold reception more than a few times. He once said, "As a child I was also lowly, so I could perform many humble duties," meaning that he came from humble origins and worked at many lowly and insignificant occupations. For instance, Confucius had worked as a petty official in charge of livestock reproduction and served as a warehouse manager. Although his duties were limited, Confucius performed outstandingly and never felt inferior because of the minor role of his jobs.

Due to his modesty, politeness, scope of knowledge, and good memory, Confucius was gradually recognized by many and caught the attention of the upper class in Lu. Some nobles and officials came to consult Confucius, and some became his students. When the son of Confucius was born, the duke of Lu sent an envoy to present a carp as a congratulatory gift, so Confucius named his son Kong Li [lit., "carp"]. Soon afterwards, Confucius went to the capital of the Zhou kingdom at the recommendation of the duke of Lu to study the Zhou rites. During his sojourn in the capital, Confucius had the opportunity to meet with the great scholar Laozi, founder of Daoism. Confucius also personally witnessed all kinds of Zhou rituals and read some of the relevant literature. This experience prepared Confucius for his later career in politics and teaching while laying a foundation for the monumental task of compiling the Chinese Classics. He had finally found the kind of work and career that would suit him.

"By thirty, one gets established," he once concluded, meaning that at age thirty, one should have become established in life with a suitable job or career.

In 501 BCE, Confucius gained his first official post when he was appointed magistrate of Zhongdu (*Zhongdu zai*). He was fifty-one at the time, and Zhongdu was a small city in Lu. The magistrate of Zhongdu was the top post of that locality. During the short period under Confucius's administration, the area was transformed into one where "things left on the sidewalk would not vanish," and it became a role model for other localities to follow. The merit of Confucius was recognized by the ruler, and he was promoted to the Lu minister of works in charge of building and road construction. Soon afterwards, he was promoted again to minister of justice in charge of law enforcement. Confucius began to share responsibility with state secretaries and served as acting premier. He had become one of the core members of the decision-making Lu state cabinet. During this period, there were two events that brought him fame. One was the Jiagu Conference, which was a diplomatic summit meeting between Qi and Lu attended by both heads of state. The powerful Qi state had intended to take this opportunity to humiliate Lu and threaten it into submission. But Confucius denounced Qi with his speeches about righteousness and his broad knowledge of correct ritual, and in the end Qi agreed to return territories taken from Lu. The duke of Qi even made an apology to the duke of Lu. This incident created the miracle of victory by a weaker nation through foreign diplomacy. The second event was the "purge of the three powerful clans," the families of Jisun, Shusun, and Mengsun, which had long dominated the politics of Lu. This move weakened the power of the three families and consolidated that of the ruler. However, some of Confucius's measures worked against the interests of the Lu nobility, and he was forced to resign. Seeking to realize his political ideals, Confucius left the state of Lu and embarked on a long set of campaign journeys, traveling with his students from state to state.

Actually Confucius traveled through only the following six states: Wei, Chen, Cao, Song, Zheng, and Cai. These states were mainly located in the present-day provinces of Henan and Shandong. He spent a total of fourteen years traveling and sojourning in these six states, "preaching his ideals" (*xingdao*) and "seeking office" (*qiushi*). "To preach his ideals" was to campaign for his political beliefs of governing through "benevolence and virtue" (*rende*). "To seek office" was to secure an official position. Only when one is in office can one have the opportunity to govern the country based on one's own political ideals. His travel experiences were not smooth at all; they were in fact disappointing. Although Confucius was received with more than adequate respect from the dukes of all the states he visited, they showed little interest in his political ideals. Confucius was not able to achieve his objectives during his long campaign travels from state to state; he did, however, gradually perfect his system of thought on these journeys. Along with his disciples, he laid the foundation for the doctrines of the Confucian school (*rujia*).

After receiving an invitation from the duke of Lu, Confucius returned to his home state when he was sixty-eight years old. Upon his return to his hometown, Qufu, he was honored as Grand Master of the State, marking an end to his campaign travels. Confucius spent the rest of his life compiling the Classics and teaching. The books that Confucius edited and collated include the *Book of Odes*, the *Book of Documents*, the *Book of Rites*, the *Book of Music*, the *Book of Changes*, and the *Spring and Autumn Annals*. These works are also called the Six Classics or the Six Noble Arts. They serve as guides in the study of traditional Chinese culture and are an invaluable part of China's cultural heritage. They were to become fundamental textbooks for the entire Chinese nation and influence the Far East for more than two thousand years. Confucius was an untiring educator who taught more than three thousand students in his lifetime. Among them, many were outstanding disciples who were to have great impact on society. In addition to the compilation of books and educating students, Confucius was a perpetual learner even in his old age. He was said to have referenced the *Book of Changes* so frequently that the strings of the bamboo strips had to be replaced three times. This is the famous story known as "three replacements of the strings in the bamboo book."

In 479 BCE, Confucius died of illness. On the life of Confucius, the famous Han dynasty grand historian Sima Qian left an apt comment: "Under heaven, kings and saints are numerous. During their own time, all had their glory. But the name of Confucius, a man of no rank, has been transmitted for more than ten generations, and scholars revere him [as an ancestor]. From the son of heaven, kings, and marquises [on down], all those in the Middle Kingdom who speak of the Six Noble Arts find the 'middle way' in Confucius. What an ultimate sage!" As a matter of fact, the spirit of personal integrity of Confucius has lasted much longer than "ten generations." After more than two millennia, it still shines.

The Philosophy of Confucius

Confucius is the most outstanding thinker in Chinese history. His main ideas are preserved in the book *Lunyu*, or *Analects*, compiled from the writings of his disciples and later generations of students after Confucius's death. Its main contents are records of dialogues between Confucius and his disciples, discussions between the disciples, as well as conversations between Confucius and other people. The *Analects* has had a tremendous impact on the course of China's history. There is a saying, "Read half of the *Analects*, and you are equipped to run the whole country."

The profundity of the Confucian philosophical system is overwhelming. But its core values are mainly reflected in its emphasis on the two aspects benevolence (*ren*) and rites (*li*).

Benevolence is the cardinal principle of Confucian thought and also the greatest attainment of human virtue. Throughout his life, Confucius tried to expound on the meaning of benevolence and tried to see the ideologies based on his beliefs implemented. There are three aspects to the concept of *ren*. First, he who is benevolent is kind. It requires that people love each other and live in unity. The second is "self-cultivation" (*xiushen*), which requires conscientious following of moral principles. As long as everyone is aware of the need to exercise self-discipline in order to maintain good ethics, society as a whole will be full of love, a necessary step towards the final restoration of "grand benevolence to all under heaven." The third is "humanism" (*renben*), i.e., to place people first or above all else. In the *Analects* we read that there was a fire in a stable, and Confucius's first concern was whether anybody was hurt. This small incident reflects the meaning of *ren* in the Confucian doctrine, that caring for people is of the utmost concern. What separates humans from animals is that humans have a sense of morality. What separates a gentleman from an ordinary human being is that the gentleman maintains his moral values conscientiously.

The original meaning of the term "rites" (*li*) encompassed politics, ethics, and standards of moral conduct. It refers to the most important norms of social behavior, rather than its modern meaning of mere politeness. There are two aspects to the concept of rites: first, the sense of awe and respect (*jing*) for ancestors and gods and, second, the actual process of the ritual ceremonies. A set of sacrificial formalities were established during the Western Zhou period (ca. 1050–771 BCE); it was known as the *Rites of Zhou* (*Zhouli*), the country's great canon of governance. Matching these stately formalities were the *Etiquette and Rites* (*Yili*), which served as standards of conduct for the people. Based on their study and interpretations of these two ritual classics, Confucian scholars of later dynasties combined them into a compilation known as the *Record of Rites* (*Liji*). These three texts came to be called the Three Books of Rites (*Sanli*), a complete suite for successive Chinese dynasties and courts to implement as the orthodox etiquette of imperial ceremonies.

Confucius loved and observed rituals and etiquette which were based on those of the Zhou dynasty. At age seventeen, he was already known in Lu for his knowledge of the rituals. Afterwards, his three thousand students and some seventy outstanding followers brought him great respect. Other disciples of Confucianism inherited the theories of rites that Confucius so strongly advocated. However, in an era of "corrupted rites and broken music" such as the Spring and Autumn and the Warring States periods, the immediate concerns of the rulers were how to strengthen the army and enrich their states. Most of them settled their disputes by resorting to force. Therefore, the ideals of Confucius were not accepted nor practiced by any of the vassal states during his lifetime. Not until the Western Han period did the emperors begin to realize the importance of Confucian philosophy in maintaining social order. The realization that a person's role, rank, or place in society could be clearly defined and made explicit for everyone to follow and that it could help in maintaining domestic stability and in running state affairs prompted the rulers to "honor only Confucianism."

In addition to benevolence and rites, the book *Doctrine of the Mean* (*Zhongyong*) is also an important part of Confucian thought. To follow the "golden mean" is to be unbiased or detached, neither left nor right. The Doctrine of the Mean is a mode of thinking, as well as a philosophy of life. It encourages people to restrain themselves in self-cultivation, to avoid going to extremes, to remain unbiased, and to make the right amount of response to any situation. Mao Zedong had at one time raised the Doctrine of the Mean to the height of a philosophy. Confucius had an adage that "too much is the same as not enough," which applies to both work and interpersonal relations. Neither situation is desired. The above saying was used by Confucius when he was asked which of his students, Zizhang or Zixia, was the better. Confucius thought that Zizhang went overboard and Zixia came up short of what was expected. Therefore, both had room for improvement. Neither was better or worse than the other. The moral of the story is to avoid extremes in dealing with any situation. The "golden mean" is achieved only after proper adjustment has been made, balancing the pros and cons just the right amount.

Confucius also proposed the idea of *he er butong* (lit., "harmony but not the same"), or "existing in harmony while maintaining differences," another aspect of the Doctrine of the Mean. Harmony was a kind of situation sought after by Confucius. There should be harmony among people. Man should exist in harmony with nature. Conflicts should be avoided. "Same" (*tong*) means no difference. Human societies are colorfully diverse, so it is impossible to have no difference. However, under the premise of harmony, people can keep their own differences. This is the principle of "existing in harmony while maintaining differences" that was advocated by Confucius.

Whether it is the concept of benevolence, the practice of rites, or the Doctrine of the Mean, the ultimate goal is a "grand harmony," or the grand harmony of all under heaven. In Confucian thought, an ideal society in a grand harmony is one where "The world belongs to everybody" (i.e. there is something for everyone, when an effort is made by all under heaven). Confucius once said:

> When the Great *Dao* prevails, the ethical vision of public interest is shared by all under heaven. Men of virtue and ability are chosen to run a society where words mean trust and deeds cultivate harmony so that men love not only their own families nor treat as children only their own children. Thus the aged till their death are secured with provisions. The able-bodied are employed to the extent of their capacity. Widowers, widows, orphans, the childless, the disabled, and the sick— all are taken care of with compassion. Males take their share of responsibilities, and females have their families. To throw away goods on the ground would be considered a shame. To keep accumulating stuff for oneself would be deemed unnecessary. To work only towards one's own advantage but otherwise refuse participation would be despised. For fewer reasons in development, schemes are reduced. Robbers, burglars, and rebellious traitors are curbed. Therefore the front doors don't have to be shut. This is an era when grand harmony is achieved.

In general, benevolence addresses individual cultivation while rites deal with social order. Politically,

these principles call for administrators to rule by benevolence, to govern by implementation of rites, to maintain order by instilling respect, to promote education and good virtue, to repress violence, and work towards establishing well-to-do families and an ideal society in great harmony. In education, start with benevolence and caring, and teach by instilling a moral sense and good virtue. Education should be made universal for all children, and easy access be provided to the masses. Both virtue and talent are to be qualities for candidates when choosing leaders. In social ethics, use benevolence as content and proper rituals as form in the establishment of a complete system of ethics. The basic standards of human morality were also identified by Confucius as the following: "loyalty, filial piety, benevolence, righteousness, rites, wisdom, and trust" and "being moderate, law abiding, respectful, thrifty, and polite." From individuals to society to the state, the comprehensive set of political guidelines and socio-ethical rules used for self-cultivation, governing, and maintaining a peaceful realm in Confucianism has become a model for later generations.

Confucius was a great educator and the first ever to run a private school. Since then, there have been two modes of education in China: private or government-run. Unlike education policies set by feudal institutions, Confucius advocated "education for all without distinction." As long as people are willing to learn, he would accept them. This practice changed a situation in which education was monopolized by the aristocracy. Many more people could now benefit. According to stories, he had more than 3,000 students, among whom seventy-two were most accomplished. Those most frequently mentioned nowadays include: Zeng Shen, Zixia, Zizhang, Zilu, Zeng Xi, and Ran You. They serve as testimony to the success of Confucius's approach to education. He left us with a wealth of famous sayings on education and learning, such as the following:

> Review the old to understand the new.
> Learn. And practice what has been learned frequently.
> Learning without thought is a snare; thinking without learning is a danger. (One is encouraged to combine learning with active thinking.)
> When you know a thing, acknowledge that you do; when you don't, admit it.
> Never be satiated with learning.

> There is no shame in asking questions and learning
> from one's subordinates.
> Traveling in a group of three, there must be a teacher
> for me. Identify their good qualities to follow
> suit and their bad habits to correct them.
> From one instance, draw three inferences. (This
> refers to both attitude as well as way of learning.)

And there are those sayings that emphasize the moral righteousness of the student: "Don't do to others what you do not want done to yourself"; "think it over three times before you act"; "the great man is not a mere receptacle"; "be poor and happy, rich and courteous"; and "be true to your words, and make sure they yield results."

His greater emphasis was, of course, on benevolence and rites in education and training of qualified persons the state can use. Due to the huge impact and achievements of Confucius in education, he has been called the "Sacred Model Teacher through the Ages," a title he certainly deserves.

The current world is constantly marred by disputes which from time to time lead to war. Despite the high level of civilization today, loathsome events still occur. In dealing with problems of modern society, such as personal ethics, work ethics, and interpersonal as well as international relations, and in working out our cultural differences and conflicts, sagely advice can still be found in the 2,500-year-old wisdom of Confucius. This is the benefit for a modern society in learning about Confucius and his thoughts.

THE CITY OF QUFU AND ITS RELICS RELATING TO CONFUCIUS

Located in the southwestern part of Shandong province, Qufu has a history of over five thousand years and is known as the "Sacred City of the East." It is a county-level city where a quarter of its population has Kong as the family name. A place with "thousand-year-old rites and music originated from east of Lu and where ancient dukes and kings came to honor the uncrowned king [Confucius]," Qufu has enjoyed world recognition due to its association with the name of Confucius. During the long course of over two thousand years of history, Confucian culture has become China's orthodox culture and has influenced countries of East Asia and Southeast Asia, making it a cultural foundation for the entire Far East. Known collectively as the "Three Kong," the Temple of Confucius (Kongmiao) in Qufu, the Kong Family Mansion (Kongfu), and the Cemetery of Confucius, or

Kong Cemetery (Konglin), embody the great veneration for Confucius and the promotion of his idealogy in China for successive generations. They are renowned for their rich cultural heritage, long history, impressive scale, and large collections of relics with scientific significance and artistic value. Due to their prominence in Chinese history and in Eastern cultures, they were incorporated by UNESCO as a World Heritage Site. In December 1994, they were entered into the World Heritage List, and Qufu became one of mankind's three sacred cities.

The Temple of Confucius

The Temple of Confucius is located inside the city of Qufu. Its buildings are magnificent in scale and splendidly decorated. The largest ceremonies in memory of Confucius in China are held here. In 478 BCE, the year after Confucius's death, Duke Ai of Lu consecrated his former residence as a temple. Emperors of successive dynasties have bestowed title upon title on Confucius and added buildings to the complex. In the Qing dynasty, the Yongzheng emperor (r. 1723–35) ordered a great renovation, and the complex was enlarged to its present size. There are nine courtyards arranged along a central north-south axis, and the buildings are arranged in three axes (left, central, and right) that stretch 630 meters in length and 140 meters in width (see diagram, opp. p. 1). There are palaces (*dian*), halls (*tang*), altars (*tan*), and pavilions (*ge*), totaling more than 460 rooms; fifty-four gates; and the Thirteen Imperial Stele Pavilions. Along the central axis are the Star of Literature Pavilion (Kuiwen'ge), the thirteen stele pavilions, the Apricot Platform, and the Hall of Great Accomplishment (Dachengdian). There is a large collection of steles and carved stone tablets in the Hall of the Sage's Traces (Shengjidian), the thirteen stele pavilions, and two galleries flanking the Hall of Great Accomplishment. The best collection of Han steles, the largest of its kind in the nation, is to be found here. Some masterpieces in the history of carved steles are also found here, as well as lesser known examples. By quantity, this is the second largest stele collection after that of the Stele Forest in Xi'an. So it is also known as Stele Forest Number Two.

The main building of the Temple of Confucius is the Hall of Great Accomplishment, which serves as the architectural core of the whole complex. Previously known as the Temple of the Declared Lord of Letters (Wenxuanwang dian) in the Tang dynasty (618–907), the complex had five rooms at that time. During the overhaul in 1021 (5th year of the Song dynasty Tianxi reign), the complex was moved to its current location and

expanded into seven halls. In commemoration of
Confucius's achievements, Song emperor Huizong (Zhao
Ji) in 1104 (3rd year of the Chongning era) picked a few
characters from the following line in the book of *Mencius*,
Kongzi zhiwei ji dacheng (Confucius can be called an
epitomizer of all schools), and issued a decree to have the
name of the main hall changed to the Hall of Great
Accomplishment. In 1724 (2nd year of the Qing dynasty
Yongzheng era), the hall was rebuilt with new features
such as a nine-ridged hip roof with double eaves, yellow-
glazed roof tiles, carved beams and pillars, and an
octagonal caisson ceiling decorated with a colored dragon
motif. A vertical tablet hung at the center of one of the
double cornices bears three carved and gilt characters
reading "Hall of Great Accomplishment" in the calligraphy
of the Yongzheng emperor. The hall stands 24.8 meters
high, 45.69 meters wide, and 24.85 meters deep. Sitting on
a 2.1-meter-high raised base, this hall is the tallest of all
the buildings in the complex and also one of the three
most famous ancient palace structures in the nation.

In the middle of the courtyard on the paved path
leading to the Hall of Great Accomplishment is the
Apricot Platform, marking the spot where Confucius
frequently lectured to his students. Next to the platform
is an ancient cypress said to have been "hand planted by
the First Teacher." The platform has vermilion columns
and handrails all around. The hip-and-gable roof with
crossed ridges is topped with two tiers of yellow-glazed
tiles placed over double semi-brackets. Inside the
building is a caisson ceiling elaborately decorated with
colored paintings and gold coiled dragons. Housed under
its roof is a stone tablet carved with the characters *xing
tan zan* (In praise of the Apricot Platform) in the
calligraphy of the Qing dynasty Qianlong emperor
(r. 1736–95). Next to the platform stands a stone incense
burner, approximately one meter in height. Archaic in
shape, it is a relic from the Jin dynasty (1115–1234).

The Kong Family Mansion

Adjacent to the Temple of Confucius on its east is the
Kong Family Mansion (fig. 1), the private residence of the
Duke for Perpetuating the Sage (*Yanshenggong*) of various
generations and their male lineal descendants. The
mansion is second in scale only to the Ming and Qing
imperial residences. Currently the Kong Family Mansion
covers an area of 240 *mu* (39.5 acres) and has many types
of buildings, including offices (*ting*), halls (*tang*), storied
buildings (*lou*), and studios (*xuan*), totaling 463 rooms.
The buildings are arranged in three axes from east to west.

Fig. 1. Entrance to the Kong Family Mansion. Photo courtesy of
The Confucius Museum in Qufu, Shandong Province

The eastern axis comprises the family temple; the western
axis houses an academy; and the central axis is lined with
main buildings and offices. Living quarters are in the rear
of the central axis, separated from the offices in the front.
The buildings in the front include three halls and six
offices. (They are the Great Hall, the Second Hall, and
the Third Hall. The offices are the Office of Taxation, the
Office of Contractors, the Office of Seals and Authentication,
the Office of Books, the Office of Archives, and the Office
of Music.) At the back, the inner living quarters include
the Front Reception Room, the Front Hall Building, the
Rear Hall Building, the Rear Five Rooms, and finally the
Kong Family Garden where successive generations of the
Duke for Perpetuating the Sage spent their leisure time
with family members.

The Great Hall is where the Duke held public
sessions. The hall has a "chamber of eight-treasures,"
armchairs upholstered with tiger skin, and a red lacquer
desk upon which sits an official seal, command flags and
warrant arrows, a gavel, and the four treasures of the

Fig. 2. Entrance gate to the Cemetery of Confucius. Photo courtesy of The Confucius Museum in Qufu, Shandong Province

scholar's studio. Standing on both sides of the hall are the guards, looking solemn and formidable.

The furnishings and items in the former residence of Kong Lingyi (see cat. no. 30), the seventy-sixth-generation Duke for Perpetuating the Sage, are still intact. Large quantities of historical relics are in the private collection of the Kong family. The most famous among them are the Ten Ceremonial Vessels of the Shang and Zhou Dynasties (cat. no. 23), or simply the Ten Ceremonial Vessels, formerly in the imperial collection, presented as gifts to the Kong family in 1771 by the Qianlong emperor.

The Cemetery of Confucius
Originally known as the "Sacred Forest," the Cemetery of Confucius is located to the north of Qufu's city center. Belonging to the Kong family, it is the largest and oldest private burial ground of a single family clan in the world (fig. 2). Confucius died in the fourth month of 479 BCE (16th year in the reign of Duke Ai of Lu) and was buried on the northern bank of the Si River to the north of the Lu capital. Having lost both of his parents at an early age, his wife in his middle age, and his son in his old age, Confucus had experienced all of what is known as the five utmost miseries in the life of an individual. Therefore, he left a wish to have himself buried next to his deceased son. His grandson was placed opposite to him, so he was finally in a position where he could "hold the son by the hand and the grandson in his arm." His descendants were buried around him generation after generation until the cemetery reached its present scale.

Originally, Confucius's tomb had no tumulus. By the Qin and Han dynasties, a mound was built over the tomb. However, the lot was still small, and several households of graveyard attendants lived around it. With the increased status of Confucius, the cemetery became progressively larger. In 157 (3rd year of the Yongshou era under Emperor Huan of the Eastern Han), Prime Minister Han of Lu ordered the renovation of Confucius's tomb; a gate was erected in front of the tomb, a house built for sacrifices to the southeast, and several families headed by Wu Chu were stationed there to attend to the graveyard and offer sacrifices. The area covered by the Confucius Cemetery at that time "was shy of one hectare." By the Southern and Northern Dynasties period, when the Gao clan ruled the Qi state, there were only six hundred trees planted. During the Song dynasty Xuanhe reign period (1119–25), stone figures were added in front of the tomb.

In 1331, Kong Sikai set up the perimeter wall and built gates to the cemetery. In 1684, the Cemetery of Confucius was expanded to three thousand *mu* (494 acres). In 1730, an overhaul of the cemetery was carried out in which 25,300 *liang* (44,621 oz.) of silver were spent to redo the gates and officials were sent to guard the place. According to statistics, there have been thirteen renovation projects and expansions since the Han dynasty (206 BCE–220 CE), five large scale plantings of trees, and three enlargements of forested areas. The perimeter wall now measures 7.25 kilometers in length, over three meters in height, and about five meters in thickness. The cemetery covers an area of two square kilometers, which is larger than the ancient city of Qufu itself.

At the Kong family cemetery, burial activities had not ceased in the past two millennia. Preserved here are verifiable burials of the Spring and Autumn period and documented tombs of the Qin and Han dynasties, providing a great resource for the study of political, economic, and cultural developments and the evolution of burial customs in China. In 1961, the State Council announced the first batch of Protected Key National Cultural Heritage Sites, and this cemetery was included.

The poetic lines, "For millennia the ancient tomb has been there / It's the month of May, the forest remains chill" capture the setting. Since the time that the disciple Zigong set up a dwelling on the graveyard of Confucius and planted some trees, the number of ancient trees in the cemetery has reached over ten thousand. According to legend, "disciples started planting exotic woods from all over, resulting in a great variety of unusual trees. Some of the trees have never been identified by the local people of the Lu state." Still today, there are trees in the Cemetery of Confucius that people don't know how to name. The identified trees include cypress, Chinese juniper, elm, pagoda tree (Sophora), Chinese pistache, hackberry, maple, poplar, willow, sandalwood, privet, Chinese magnolia vine, and cherry; they are all deeply rooted and have gnarled branches with luxuriant foliage. There are also nearly several hundred types of plants that thrive seasonally: daisies, Pinellia tubers, Starwort, Heterophylly false starwort, Ganoderma (*lingzhi*), Tuber fleece flowers, and so on. The Cemetery of Confucius is indeed like a natural botanical garden.

THE KONG FAMILY ARCHIVES
AND THE CONFUCIUS MUSEUM

The Kong Family Mansion is also known as the Residence of the Duke for Perpetuating the Sage (Yanshenggong fu). This elite title is hereditary and has been unaffected by the waxing and waning of imperial power or dynastic changes. Due to its privilege, the Kong family has been able to preserve a large family archive that is relatively complete. A great amount of official correspondence between the Kong family and the court or imperial institutions can be found in it. Much of the documents bear evidence of the interdependent relationship as well as conflicts of interest between the feudal courts and aristocratic landlords. There are also records of tenant protests against duties and rents. Dating from 1534 to 1937, a span of over four hundred years, the current archives at the Residence of the Duke contains more than 200,000 documents. The great wealth of information preserved by this collection is crucial to studies in institutional politics, economics, ideology, and patriarchal rules and regulations in the later periods of imperial China.

These archives were originally indexed into several categories by the Kong family in the order of the first few characters of the "Thousand-Character Text": *tian, di, xuan, huang, yu, zhou, hong, huang*. There was no sub-index. Stored loosely in several locations, some were dust-laden, and others were left susceptible to damage by mildew. Due to the private nature of the archives, they had remained unknown to the public. After 1949 when the Qufu City Cultural Relics Administration Committee was established, all documents were systematically categorized and re-indexed into some nine thousand volumes under the guidance of experts from the National Archives.

After Confucius died, his residence was "consecrated as a temple" for people to worship on important occasions. His descendants in the Kong family resided next to the temple. In 195, when Emperor Gaozu of Han visited Qufu to pay homage to Confucius, he conferred the title of Sacrificial Officer on Kong Teng, the ninth-generation male lineal descendant, who was to be in charge of the sacrificial ceremonies. Ever since then, titles of honor, different in wording but same in function, have been conferred on the lineal descendants of Confucius. By the Northern Song dynasty (in 1055), the title of Duke for Perpetuating the Sage was conferred on Kong Zongyuan, the forty-sixth-generation lineal descendant. This title was to last until the end of the Qing dynasty. In 1935, the title was changed to State Master of Sacrifice to the Most Venerated Sage and First Teacher.

During the Northern Song, a special area of jurisdiction, complete with a civil court, had been established on the Kong family estate, where a hereditary "Supervisor" was installed by imperial decree along with officials appointed to various posts. Ming and Qing imperial decrees defined the estate as the Prefecture of the Duke for Perpetuating the Sage and established sub-levels of officials whose uniforms and costumes were designed according to their rank. They were assigned to protect the temple, take charge of the sacrificial vessels, and manage the estate fields and tenant households. Sacrificial ceremonies in memory of Confucius were held throughout the four seasons.

In August of 1948, the Institute for the Preservation of Relics from the Kong Family Mansion was established. In March of 1949, it was changed to the Qufu City Cultural Relics Administration Committee, and in March of 1994, it was renamed the Museum of Confucius (*Kongzi bowuyuan*). At the beginning of the 21st century, an expansion project was proposed to build a Confucius Museum (*bowuguan*) with a total land area of 130 *mu* (21.4 acres) and 60,000 square meters of architectural structure. Based on the need for different functions, the Confucius Museum will have the following seven areas or departments: exhibitions, public relations, education, visitor services, conservation, security, and fire safety. There will be eight permanent exhibitions, including the Hall of Qufu City History, Hall of Fine Cultural Relics Collection, Stele Forest, and Hall of Stone Carvings.

There will be one hall for featured temporary exhibitions. The twelve categories of collections will include bronze vessels, jade objects, porcelain and ceramics, painting and calligraphy, costumes, and metalware. The museum's collection of approximately ten thousand items comes mainly from the old estate collection of the Kong Family Mansion. They include costumes of the Ming and Qing dynasties, gifts to the Temple of Confucius, steles from the Cemetery of Confucius, portraits of Confucius and his descendants, the Kong family archives, and cultural relics unearthed from the ancient Lu capital. In addition, the Confucius Museum will have five multi-purpose halls for international cultural exchange.

(Translated by David Huiwei Shen)

孔子和孔子文化

中国古代伟大的思想家、政治家、教育家孔子于公元前551年诞生于鲁国国都（今山东省曲阜市），卒于公元前479年。公元前501年，孔子走上仕途，先后任"中都宰"，鲁国的"司空"和"司寇"，并摄相事。后来他仕途不利，便率弟子出游列国，到过卫国、陈国、曹国、宋国、郑国、蔡国（在今天的河南、山东一带）。孔子没能实现自己的政治理想，却在周游中完善了自己的思想体系，和弟子们一起，奠定了"儒家"学说基础。

孔子68岁时，受鲁国国君的邀请，回到曲阜，他晚年主要把精力倾注在整理文献和教书传业。孔子先后编校了《诗》、《书》、《礼》、《乐》、《易》、《春秋》六部古典著作，这些文献成为中华民族的经典教科书，影响了东方两千多年。

春秋战国时期，形成了"百家争鸣"的局面。最著名的有孔子创立的"儒家"，老子创立的"道家"，墨子创立的"墨家"、孙子领衔的"兵家"，以及"法家"、"名家"、"农家"、"刑家"等等"诸子百家"。几乎与孔子同时，在希腊文明中产生了像苏格拉底、柏拉图、亚里斯多德等一批大思想家。乔达摩·悉达多则在古印度地区创立了佛教，并被佛教信仰者视为"佛祖"。因此，孔子诞生的时代是世界思想文化的一个爆发时期，无论是中国的孔子思想，还是欧洲希腊文明、古印度佛教，至今仍然影响着世界范围内的人们和社会。

孔子的主要思想保存在《论语》这部著作当中。"仁"是孔学的核心。孔子毕生所致力的就是阐释"仁"，主张"仁政"。其含义主要有三方面：一是"仁者爱人"，人与人之间要"亲爱团结"；二是"修身"，只要人人都能做到修身自洁，社会就会充满爱，达到"天下归仁"；三是"人本"，以人为本。

"礼"是孔学对政治、伦理、道德的总称，是最重要的社会行为规范。其内容包含两部分，一是对祖先神明的"敬"，二是祭祀的具体仪式和程序。在"礼崩乐坏"的春秋战国之际，孔子的思想并不为各诸侯国接受。直到西汉，皇帝才发现儒家的社会礼仪秩序的重要性，公元134，汉武帝接受"罢黜百家、独尊儒术"的提议，将儒家思想奉为治国之道。

中庸也是孔子思想的重要部分。"中庸"就是"不偏不倚"，是一种思想方法，也是一种人生的态度，要求人们不激进，不偏颇。孔子还提到"和而不同"，"和"就是"和谐"，人与人之间、人与自然之间要和，避免争斗；人类社会丰富多彩，不可能没有差异，在"和"的前提下，人们保持各自的差异。无论是仁、礼，还是中庸、和，孔子理想的最终目标是"大同"，"大同"社会是"天下为公"。

孔子是中国最早开办私立学校的人，他主张"有教无类"，只要愿意学习的人，都招收到自己的门下。他的学生有三千多人，其中有72人最为杰出。孔子有很多教育格言，如"温故而知新"，"学而时习之"，"学而不思则罔，思而不学则殆"，"知之为知之，不知为不知"，"学而不厌"，"不耻下问"，"三人行，必有我师焉。择其善者从之，其不善者而改之"，"举一反三"，等等。他也极力培养学生个人的修养，"己所不欲，勿施于人"，"三思而后行"，"君子不器"，"贫而乐，富而好礼"，"言必信，行必果"，等等。

自汉代平帝时封孔子为"褒成宣尼公"，唐代加封为"文宣王"，宋代仁宗皇帝把"文宣王"改为"衍圣公"，历代延续不衰，对孔子顶礼膜拜。曲阜的孔庙为中国最大的祭孔之地；孔府是孔子世袭"衍圣公"的世代嫡裔子孙居住的地方，是中国仅次于明、清皇帝宫室的最大府第；孔林是孔子及其家族的专用墓地，也是目前世界上延时最久，面积最大的氏族墓地；它们统称"三孔"，是中国历代纪念孔子，推崇儒学的表征。以其悠久历史、丰厚的文化积淀、宏大的建筑规模、丰富的文物档案珍藏，以及独特的科学艺术价值而著称，被联合国教科文组织列为世界文化遗产，于1994年12月被收入《世界遗产名录》。曲阜也被世人尊崇为世界三大圣城之一。

周晓陆　编写

Detail, fig. 1

More than One Confucius at a Time: Teacher, Statesman, God

Julia K. Murray

If one person could be said to symbolize Chinese civilization throughout the world, it would have to be the ancient thinker, teacher, and statesman called Kong Qiu or Kongzi, who is better known in the West as Confucius (551–479 BCE). Even though he died almost 2500 years ago, Confucius has been venerated as China's patron saint of learning for many centuries. As Grand Scribe Sima Qian (145–86 BCE) put it in the Han dynasty (206 BCE–220 CE), ten generations after Confucius's lifetime, "Scholars offer him cult" (xuezhe zong zhi).[1] Besides providing a model of individual self-cultivation, Confucius's teachings offered lofty ideals of governance for over two thousand years of dynastic rule. Throughout much of Chinese history, Confucius has been revered as a great teacher, preserver of ancient learning, paragon of moral conduct, upright official, and sage. Other countries of East Asia adopted portions of his teachings, and his influence is felt even today. Although we cannot hope to recover the historical Confucius at this far remove in time and space, we can begin to grasp his significance as we trace the many ways he has been viewed over the centuries.[2]

THE LIFE AND LEGACY OF CONFUCIUS

Born into humble circumstances in 551 BCE, Confucius grew up on the eastern edge of the crumbling Zhou empire in the small city-state of Lu, centered around modern-day Qufu. In ancient times, Lu had been the domain of the Duke of Zhou, who was renowned for serving loyally and wisely as regent for a young king in the precarious early years of the Zhou dynasty (ca. 1050–256 BCE). Confucius greatly admired the duke for creating the ceremonial institutions and sacrificial rites of the Zhou. Studying them from an early age, he aspired to revive them from the neglect into which they had fallen by his own day. However, his efforts to persuade contemporary dukes to return to the ancient ways met with little success. Although Confucius held a series of minor offices in his home state and for a brief period

served as a minister of justice (dasikou), with the added responsibilities of a prime minister, he eventually became frustrated with conditions in Lu.

In his middle age, Confucius left home to travel among the contending feudal states of North China, searching for an ideal ruler who would govern with benevolence and according to proper ritual. Although some leaders initially gave him an enthusiastic reception, they inevitably failed to meet his demanding standards, causing him to resume his search. After braving the dangers of the road and wandering from state to state for fourteen years, Confucius returned to Lu on the promise of gaining a substantive position at last. When his hopes were thwarted yet again, he abandoned the quest and devoted himself completely to scholarship from his late sixties onward.

While editing texts that eventually became known as the "Confucian Classics," Confucius attracted an ever-growing following, eventually comprising some seventy-two intimate disciples and three thousand others who were less close. After his death at age seventy-two, his most devoted disciples observed three years of mourning as if for a father. Some took up residence near the burial site, and Confucius's own house became a memorial shrine, the precursor to the great Temple of Confucius (Kongmiao) in Qufu today. When Sima Qian made a pilgrimage to the area during the Han dynasty, he reported that the temple still housed Confucius's personal effects, including his clothing, carriage, and ritual implements.[3]

The immediate disciples of Confucius and their students, his descendants, and later scholars all played important roles in creating early impressions of who Confucius was and what he taught. They transmitted and developed his teachings, which were later gathered into the Analects (Lunyu; literally, "Discussions and Discourses"), an influential collection of Confucius's pronouncements and dialogues with disciples, rulers, and assorted other people. His biography was first compiled by Sima Qian, who drew on varied sources and oral traditions to create a chronological account of Confucius's

Fig. 1. Anonymous, *Two Dragons and Five Old Men in the Clouds Foreshadow Confucius's Birth*. Ming dynasty, late 16th century. Leaf 3 from the album *Traces of the Sage (Pictorial Biography of Confucius)* (cat. no. 4); ink and color on silk, 33 × approx. 60 cm. The Confucius Museum in Qufu, Shandong Province

life and an outline of his family tree.[4] Most unusually, Sima Qian placed the narrative in the "Hereditary Houses" (*shijia*) section of the book, together with histories of the great aristocratic families that had wielded real power by virtue of their pedigrees. On purely genealogical grounds, Confucius did not belong there. Even though said to be descended from rulers of the Shang dynasty (ca. 1600–ca. 1050 BCE), his father had held only a minor post. Moreover, he fathered Confucius in his old age, in a relationship with a much younger woman that seems not to have been properly formalized.[5] But Sima Qian believed that Confucius's devotion to the way of ancient sages gave him the moral standing to be the teacher of kings. At the end of the biography, he acclaims Confucius as the "ultimate sage" (*zhisheng*).[6]

Other early texts known collectively as the "apochrypha" (*weishu*) describe supernatural elements in the events associated with the birth of Confucius.[7] After his mother prayed for a son at the shrine of Mount Ni, she received a visit from a *qilin*, a fabulous unicorn-like beast, which delivered a jade tablet that proclaimed, "The child of the essence of water will succeed the declining Zhou and become the uncrowned king" (*shuijing zi ji shuai Zhou er wei suwang*).[8] Two dragons cavorted over the house on the night before his birth, and gods hovered in the sky as he was being born, while a troupe of heavenly musicians celebrated the occasion. On the baby's chest was an inscription, "Talisman of the one created to stabilize the world" (*zhizuo ding shi fu*). These stories and others were handed down and later published by members of the Kong lineage, the recognized descendants of Confucius.[9]

The events were also often included in illustrated accounts of Confucius's life (e.g., see fig. 1), which are discussed below. (See also cat. no. 4).

Although Confucius himself did not write an explicit statement of his teachings, his disciples disseminated his ideas, and later followers, such as Mencius (Mengzi, 371–289 BCE) and Xunzi (ca. 313–ca. 238 BCE), developed them more fully.[10] Confucius placed great emphasis on the reciprocal obligations of all human relationships and on the scrupulous performance of appropriate rites and ceremonies. He believed that ancient sages had created a system of harmonious governance through proper ritual in which music played an important part, serving both to delight the spirits and express the character of the state. However, rulers of more recent times had lost their moral authority and abandoned these sagely institutions. Instead of leading by example and governing with benevolence, unprincipled local strongmen of his own day sought control through force and aggrandized themselves with inappropriate ceremonies. In order to restore order and harmony, Confucius believed, the ancient rituals had to be revived, and he devoted much effort to studying and codifying them.

Performing appropriate and timely sacrifices to the spirits of departed ancestors and heavenly forces was no mere formality but a matter of utmost importance.[11] Confucius regarded these rituals as opportunities for deeply moving encounters with the spirits. A reverent and sincere attitude was essential for serving the spirits properly, treating them as truly present. Before offering them food and wine, the sacrificer had to purify himself

14

and concentrate his mind in order to visualize the spirits coming down to receive the nourishment. Each sacrifice required a specific number of ceremonial vessels of specific kinds, as well as a liturgy that included prayers, music, and dance. A ruler whose sacrifices were correct in all these ways could commune with the spirits of his ancestors and gain blessings for the entire realm.

A modified version of Confucius's ideas was adopted into imperial ideology under the Han rulers, and in 136 BCE the emperor Wudi (r. 141–87 BCE) established professorships at court for each of the Five Confucian Classics (*Wu jing*).[12] These books became fundamental to Chinese ideas about sovereignty. The cumulative efforts of scholars and commentators elevated Confucius himself into a role-model of moral cultivation and learning. During the twelfth century, as part of the revival known as Neo-Confucianism or Learning of the Way (*Daoxue*), the great educator and ritualist Zhu Xi (1130–1200) distilled the essentials into an even more influential compilation called the *Four Books* (*Si shu*).[13] These texts were memorized by the educated elite, many of whom went on to take highly competitive civil-service examinations leading to government office. Zhu Xi also developed the idea that scholars constituted an imagined descent group (*zong*), the spiritual descendants of Confucius, and considered himself the "lineage head."[14] In 1684 the Kangxi emperor (r. 1662–1723) wrote a large-character epithet, "Model Teacher for 10,000 Generations" (*Wanshi shibiao*), in his own calligraphy to affirm Confucius's role. The following year, he had it carved on stone and distributed rubbings to temples at government schools throughout the realm.[15]

THE VENERATION OF CONFUCIUS

Long after his death, Confucius received a series of posthumous titles and honors bestowed by rulers of successive dynasties from the Han through Qing (1644–1911) and leaders of the Republic in the early twentieth century.[16] In 1 CE, the Han emperor Pingdi (r. 1 BCE–5 CE) conferred the rank of duke on Confucius, and in 739, Tang emperor Xuanzong (r. 712–56) elevated him in rank with the title King of Propagating Culture (*Wenxuanwang*). Lesser titles of nobility were awarded to his disciples and selected later Confucian scholars. However, in order to return attention to Confucius's importance as a teacher, the Ming Jiajing emperor (r. 1522–66) abolished the kingly title in 1530 and designated Confucius as Ultimate Sage and First Teacher (*Zhisheng xianshi*). Canonized disciples, later followers, interpreters, and commentators likewise lost their noble ranks and variously became correlates (*pei*), savants (*zhe*), former worthies (*xian xian*), and former scholars (*xian ru*).

Besides conferring titles and honors, successive dynasties supported sacrifices to Confucius and varying numbers of disciples and later Confucians.[17] Initially performed only in Qufu, eventually the rituals were carried out at sites around the empire. According to Sima Qian, in 195 BCE the Han emperor Gaozu (r. 206–195 BCE) made a grand sacrifice (*tailao*) consisting of an ox, sheep, and pig, along with wine and other offerings (see fig. 2).[18] Only a handful of later rulers came to Qufu to sacrifice in person, as most preferred to offer material support from afar. However, two emperors of the Qing dynasty, Kangxi and his grandson Qianlong (r. 1735–96), each made multiple visits, motivated as much by genuine veneration

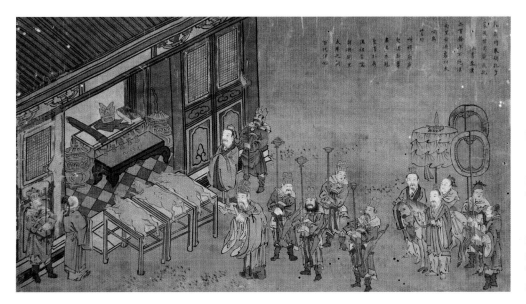

Fig. 2. Anonymous, *Han Gaozu's Sacrifice to Confucius.* Ming dynasty, late 16th century. Leaf 36 from the album *Traces of the Sage (Pictorial Biography of Confucius)* (cat. no. 4); ink and color on silk, 33 × approx. 60 cm. The Confucius Museum in Qufu, Shandong Province

Fig. 3. Hall of Great Accomplishment (Dachengdian), Temple of Confucius, Qufu, Shandong. Photo courtesy of The Confucius Museum in Qufu, Shandong Province

of the ancient sage as by a desire for the political benefits of associating the Manchu regime with his prestige by continuing the tradition of imperial patronage toward Qufu, the primordial cult site. Both rulers bestowed many precious gifts and laudatory inscriptions on the temple each time they came (see cat. no. 23).

In addition to offerings presented to Confucius in Qufu, sacrifices also began to be conducted at the imperial university (Biyong) in the capital soon after the fall of the Han dynasty.[19] In 630, the Tang emperor Taizong (r. 626–49) established a network of temples to Confucius associated with the government schools set up in provincial and prefectural centers as part of the civil service examination system. In a pattern that continued with only minor alterations under later dynasties, officials and students offered a sacrifice to Confucius and his disciples twice a year, on the first *ding* day of the second months of spring and fall.[20] The official register of state sacrifices ranked the ceremony as a middle-level rite (*zhongsi*), prescribing specific numbers and types of participants, vessels, music, foods, and other offerings to the spirits of the sage and worthies. The performance of sacrifices to Confucius was centrally supported and regulated until the end of the Qing dynasty, and observances continued in reduced and modified form even under the Republic.

THE TEMPLE OF CONFUCIUS (KONGMIAO) IN QUFU

Under the patronage of successive dynasties, the memorial shrine to Confucius in Qufu evolved into an ever larger and more magnificent Temple of Confucius (fig. 3).[21] By the mid-eighteenth century, it rivaled the imperial palace itself, with buildings organized on three south-to-north axes inside a high-walled compound (see diagram, opp. p. 1). As in the palace, most buildings are multi-bay structures with massive yellow-tiled roofs and red walls. The main axis begins with a succession of imperially inscribed commemorative arches (*paifang*) which lead to a series of gates and the multistory library, the Star of Literature Pavilion (Kuiwen'ge). Behind it are the Thirteen Imperial Stele Pavilions (Shisan Yubei ting), arranged in two rows stretching from east to west. They contain a profusion of inscribed stone tablets, often large in size, with texts written by emperors and other eminent men from the Tang (618–907) through the Qing dynasties. Additional steles occupy areas adjacent to the pavilions.

North of the stele pavilions is the courtyard of the majestic Hall of Great Accomplishment (Dachengdian), the ceremonial heart of the temple. Dragons carved in high relief adorn the stone pillars along the front of this double-roofed building, spanning a façade that is nine bays wide. Inside, festooned with imperial placards, are the altars of Confucius and his most important followers, the Four Correlates (Yan Hui, Zengzi, Zisi, and Mengzi) and Twelve Savants (eleven disciples plus Zhu Xi). They are represented by large and colorful sculptural icons as well as "spirit tablets" (*shenwei*) inscribed with their names and posthumous titles. A large paved terrace in front of the Hall of Great Accomplishment provides space for the precisely choreographed ritual dances that were part of the liturgy of sacrifice. Long corridors running down the east and west sides contain niches and altars with inscribed spirit tablets for the numerous disciples and canonized later Confucians who received auxiliary sacrifices. In the open area between the two galleries, a double-roofed pavilion called the Apricot Terrace (Xingtan) commemorates the site where Confucius taught his disciples (see cat. no. 7).[22] A majestic old juniper tree purportedly planted by Confucius himself grows nearby.

Further north, behind the Hall of Great Accomplishment stands the Resting Hall (Qindian), with the spirit tablet of Confucius's wife on the altar. The last building on the central axis is the Hall of the Sage's Traces (Shengjidian), an understated green-roofed building devoted to representational images of

Confucius.[23] Its primary display is a set of incised stone tablets illustrating a late sixteenth-century version of the life of Confucius in 112 scenes (further discussed below). The installation is complemented by assorted portrait steles and by stone tablets bearing celebratory texts by the two Qing emperors who came to Qufu. Many other imperial inscriptions appear on carved stone tablets and wooden signboards throughout the temple.

THE KONGS OF QUFU:
"FIRST FAMILY UNDER HEAVEN"

The descendants of Confucius in Qufu, surnamed Kong, also developed increasingly elaborate rituals for worshiping their illustrious ancestor. Besides serving family interests, their sacrifices to the spirit of Confucius were thought to bring blessings to the larger polity and attracted imperial support from the Han dynasty onward. Emperors conferred noble ranks and material benefits on the senior male in each generation of Kongs. Steadily elevated under later regimes, the senior male had by 1055 gained the hereditary title of Duke for Perpetuating the Sage (*Yanshenggong*), a status retained with few interruptions until 1935.[24] In addition, the Kongs received tax exemptions, hereditary offices, and agricultural lands to support their own livelihood as well as their regular sacrifices to Confucius.

Under the Ming (1368–1644) and Qing dynasties, the Duke for Perpetuating the Sage was a powerful figure who headed a large and active official establishment in Qufu, now known as the Kong Mansion (Kongfu).[25] Directly adjacent to the Temple of Confucius, the complex resembles a smaller version of the imperial palace, its high walls enclosing a stately sequence of halls and courtyards aligned on a north-south axis. Buildings for official functions and routine administration stand toward the front, and residential courtyards occupy the rear section, culminating in a well-appointed garden. Besides attending to his sacrificial responsibilities, the duke administered the financial and familial interests of the Kong lineage, corresponded with various levels of government concerning ritual matters, and received important visitors. On occasion, when required to journey to the capital in Beijing for an imperial audience, he would also deliver a lecture at the imperial university. Despite fluctuations in imperial patronage, the Kongs enjoyed a privileged position in Qufu for some two thousand years. Memorial portraits of the dukes and their wives from the middle Ming onward bear much resemblance to imperial portraiture and vividly convey

their prestigious status (see cat. nos. 26–30).[26] The Kong Mansion was filled with precious objects, paintings, and calligraphy presented by emperors and high officials (see cat. nos. 23, 34–38).

Kong descendants played important roles in creating, preserving, and reproducing images of Confucius down through the centuries. The compositions of three paintings owned and transmitted by the family were reproduced as line drawings in local gazetteers and Kong genealogies, starting with *Kongshi zuting guangji* (Expanded record of the Kong lineage), published in 1242 by Duke Kong Yuancuo (1181–ca. 1251), a fifty-first-generation descendant.[27] Additional paintings on silk or paper, some of which are displayed in the present exhibition (see cat. nos. 1, 6, 7, and 9), are recorded in a detailed inventory included in *Queli wenxian kao* (Research on documents in Queli [i.e., Qufu]), published in 1762 by sixty-ninth-generation descendant Kong Jifen (1725–1786).[28]

Members of the Kong lineage took particular care to compile and preserve records to justify their entitlements, settle controversies, and solidify their power, particularly in times of political or social dislocation.[29] They maintained a detailed biography and genealogy of Confucius, which differed somewhat from that of Sima Qian. Various Kong publications also recorded the names and titles of the main line of descendants, documented imperial bequests and proclamations, described the layout of the temple and cemetery, transcribed important stele inscriptions, and inventoried ritual paraphernalia, and sometimes included line drawings. Perhaps the best known of these compendia is the *Queli zhi* (Gazetteer of Queli) (cat. no. 3). Initially compiled in 1505 under the supervision of a provincial education official, the information was updated in later editions with a more explicit focus on Kong concerns.

Emperors who founded new dynasties or revived faltering ones typically sought to gain the allegiance of educated men by conferring additional honors on Confucius and making bequests to his temple and descendants. On occasion, competing regimes even recognized different descendants as the Kong duke. When the Song (960–1279) capital at Kaifeng suffered a devastating invasion in 1126/27 by the Jurchen Jin (1115–1234), which drove the remnants of the court out of north China, the forty-eighth-generation duke, Kong Duanyou (d. 1132), left Qufu and led some of his kinsmen to join the Song restoration in the south.[30] However, the Jin appointed his younger brother to replace him as duke in Qufu, creating a new line of succession. The Song emperor Gaozong (r. 1127–62) awarded lands and a temple to the Kong refugees in Quzhou (Zhejiang). There they reestablished their ancestral cult, and successive generations of dukes presided over a growing family base. The period of competing dukes came to an end only in the late thirteenth century, after the Mongols conquered both the Jin and the Southern Song and restored Qufu to primacy. Although the "Southern Kongs" in Quzhou no longer served as dukes and fell into obscurity for over two centuries, they eventually regained official recognition. In 1505 the Ming Zhengde emperor (r. 1505–21) ennobled the senior male of the Southern Kong lineage with a hereditary title, Hanlin Erudite of the Five Classics (*Hanlin wujing boshi*), giving him the same rank as the younger brother of the duke in Qufu.

Traditions of the Southern Kongs allege that when Kong Duanyou fled from Qufu, he brought a pair of carved wooden figurines representing Confucius and his wife, Madame Qiguan (see cat. no. 2). Carved from pistache wood (*kaimu*), the statuettes were later installed at the Quzhou temple in a building called the Pavilion for Thinking of Lu (Si Lu ge), referring to Qufu. The votive sculptures were believed to be the work of Zigong, one of the original disciples of Confucius. Renowned for keeping a six-year vigil by his master's grave, Zigong is said to have planted a pistache, also known as the "scholar's tree," which was native to his home area farther south. A petrified stump near Confucius's grave has long been identified as the remains of this tree. Many more pistaches grow throughout the cemetery, which is now called the "Kong Forest" (Konglin) or Kong Cemetery.

CONFUCIUS IN THE TWENTIETH CENTURY

Despite the close association between the veneration of Confucius and the dynastic system, Confucius did not become irrelevant after the last emperor abdicated in the early twentieth century. Some prominent reformers, such as Kang Youwei (1858–1927), promoted popular worship of Confucius and sought to make "Confucianism" (*Kongjiao*) a national religion on the model of Protestantism.[31] Others attempted to portray Confucius as China's counterpart to the West's great rational philosophers, focusing on his ideas about self-cultivation and morality. However, more radical intellectuals associated with the May Fourth Movement, such as Chen Duxiu (1879–1942), rejected Confucius along with the customs and traditions linked to his teachings, calling on the Chinese to "smash the Confucius family shop" (*dadao Kongjia dian*). Continued veneration of Confucius came to be associated with Qing loyalists, monarchists, warlords,

and conservative Nationalist leaders. In addition, the Japanese rationalized their imperialistic ambitions by claiming superior qualifications to preserve the ancient heritage and uphold Confucian traditions. Tainted by such associations, Confucius fell into disfavor on the mainland after the Communist victory in 1949.

During the Cultural Revolution of 1966 to 1976, Confucius was reviled as an arch-villain whose teachings had shackled China with feudal ideas and customs. At the height of the Red Guards' iconoclastic fervor in 1966, many temples and artifacts related to Confucius were destroyed. Even though the Temple of Confucius, Kong Mansion, and Kong Cemetery had received official designation as national cultural relics, they suffered grievous damage. In the temple, rampaging youths demolished votive sculptures and spirit tablets and pulled down countless stone steles attesting to the patronage of emperors, officials, and Kong descendants over the centuries.[32] Also, memorial stones in the Kong Cemetery were smashed or defaced, and the grave of Confucius was dug up. Many historical items in the Kong Mansion were confiscated or burned, while other treasures were buried or hidden for safekeeping.[33] The "Criticize Lin Biao, Criticize Confucius" (*Pi Lin pi Kong*) campaign of 1973–74 brought renewed attacks, this time largely verbal, on "Kong Lao'er" (Old Number-Two Kong, meaning Confucius).[34] Publications to popularize the campaign included not just single posters disparaging Confucius but also a set of linked pictures titled *The Life of the Evil Confucius* (*Kong Lao'er zui'e de yisheng*), which recast his biography and distorted his teachings beyond recognition in order to present him as distastefully as possible.[35]

With the end of the Cultural Revolution and death of Mao Zedong in 1976, a process to rehabilitate Confucius and his legacy gradually got underway. By the mid 1980s, China had established major institutes for research on Confucianism and set up a foundation to advance Confucian studies. Confucian temples that had been converted to other uses or even destroyed began being repaired or rebuilt all across the country. In 1984, Qufu hosted what has become an annual festival to celebrate September 28 as Confucius's birthday, during which a temple ceremony based on the traditional sacrifice is performed. Young students are once again memorizing the *Analects*, and the Confucian Classics are being taught in an array of institutional settings.[36] Confucius has become the theorist of social harmony and the symbol of Chinese civilization itself.[37]

VISUAL REPRESENTATIONS OF CONFUCIUS

Posthumous veneration of Confucius eventually gave rise to depictions of the ancient master in a great variety of media, including painting, incised stone tablets, woodblock prints, and sculpture in clay, wood, or metal.[38] The images reflect various beliefs concerning his personal qualities, deeds, and significance. Portrayals of Confucius as a teacher are best known, but he was also depicted as an official, and temple icons presented him in the ceremonial regalia of an emperor. A convenient way of categorizing the depictions is by the role in which he was being envisioned, which is often signaled by his headgear. A simple cloth cap is the hallmark of his career as a teacher, an official hat marks his brief service in government, and a crown refers to his posthumous elevation to king. Further distinctions can be made between representations of Confucius as a living person and as a temple icon that evolved in accord with posthumous changes in his social and ritual status.

Current evidence suggests that images of Confucius began being made during the Eastern Han period (25–220). The earliest reference appears in the bibliography of the *History of the Former Han* (*Hanshu*), compiled in the late first century. It lists the title "Method of Depicting Confucius and His Disciples" (*Kongzi turen tufa*) as a work in two scrolls (*juan*) but does not describe them, and they have not survived.[39] According to the *History of the Later Han* (*Hou Hanshu*), Cai Yong (133–192) painted Confucius and seventy-two disciples on the walls of the Hongdumen school in the capital at Luoyang in 178.[40] These exemplary men were also part of a larger group of mythical and historical heroes portrayed in the late second century at the Yizhou Academy in present-day Chengdu, Sichuan. Later people often credited the Yizhou images to Wen Weng (active mid-2nd c. BCE), the early Han administrator who had founded the academy to help civilize the peripheral region. Some Ming accounts even imply that the Yizhou portrait of Confucius was based on an image made close to his lifetime.[41]

A number of early representations of Confucius have survived on incised stone slabs from second-century offering shrines and tombs in southwestern Shandong, the region near his home.[42] Some portray him with several disciples standing in a long row, a formal arrangement that may have resembled the long-destroyed painted murals. Other stones depict Confucius facing Laozi, who is best known as a Daoist master, and the child Xiang Tuo; they were perhaps meant to symbolize his ability to learn from old and young alike (see cat. no. 8). Sima Qian's biography of Confucius says that he met Laozi during a visit to the capital to study Zhou rituals.[43] The much later pictorial biographies of Confucius (discussed below) invariably include a scene showing him seated in respectful conversation with an elderly Laozi (see cat. no. 4). As for Xiang Tuo, Sima Qian refers to him only in passing in another biography as the seven-year-old teacher of Confucius, but fuller details of their encounter are given in the *Huainanzi*, a text compiled around 139 BCE.[44] Nonetheless, their meeting does not appear in any of the later pictorial biographies of Confucius.

Sculptural representations of Confucius intended to provide a focus for temple rituals probably began to be made during the Period of Disunion (220–589) that followed the fall of the Han in 220.[45] The development of three-dimensional effigies owed something to the stimulus of Buddhism, which became well established during these centuries. Many Buddhist rites were performed in the presence of anthropomorphic icons, both sculptural and painted, and the concept spread to other cults, influencing practices of ancestor veneration as well. Sixth-century sources note that sculptural images were displayed in the Qufu temple, initially depicting Confucius flanked by just two disciples, a number later expanded to ten.[46] By the Tang dynasty, if not earlier, temples elsewhere had also installed sculptural icons to serve as the focus of sacrifices.

It seems likely that temple statues represented Confucius with the attributes appropriate to his posthumous status. Ranked as a king after 739, he would have been depicted with a robe displaying the requisite

Fig. 4. Altar installed with just an inscribed tablet to represent Confucius. Temple of Confucius, Tainan, Taiwan. Photo: Thomas A. Wilson

nine auspicious emblems, and his crown would have had nine strings of jade beads hanging at the front and back. By the late twelfth century, additional honors conferred by later emperors increased the number of emblems on the robe and strings of jade beads on the crown to twelve each. Seated on a throne facing south, his effigy held a jade tablet (*zhen gui*) carved with mountains rising from the waves. Visually and positionally, the "uncrowned king" had become an emperor. Such images could be found in temples of Confucius throughout China until 1530, when the Jiajing emperor abolished the posthumous titles of nobility held by Confucius, his disciples, and later scholars. In an act that is often characterized as iconoclastic, the emperor also commanded that temples associated with government schools replace all sculptural or painted representations with tablets inscribed with the name and title of each canonized figure (fig. 4).[47]

Fig. 5. Sculptural icon of Confucius. Qing dynasty, dateable to 1730 (now destroyed). Hall of Great Accomplishment (Dachengdian), Temple of Confucius, Qufu, Shandong. Photo 1942, Hedda Morrison Collection, Harvard-Yenching Library, President and Fellows of Harvard College

With the removal of anthropomorphic images in 1530, the typical Confucian temple (*wenmiao*) became an austere place, in sharp contrast with Buddhist, Daoist, and popular shrines where devotees encountered colorful figures of deities. Instead, the environment was filled with writing—small inscribed tablets on the altars and celebratory epithets and couplets in larger calligraphy hanging from beams and pillars. Moreover, only members of the educated male elite were allowed to participate in sacrificial ceremonies, whose purpose was to express reverence for the Way, represented by the entire canon of Confucian learning. Confucius was not an efficacious god who granted the wishes of supplicants, and ordinary people did not pray to him for personal benefits.[48] However, the Qufu temple and a few others belonging to the Kong lineage were allowed to keep their images. As if to draw attention to this special dispensation, later editions of *Queli zhi* include a line drawing of the Qufu icon (see cat. no. 3). The statue of Confucius reconstructed in 1984 and now installed in the Hall of Great Accomplishment faithfully preserves the features of earlier versions (fig. 5).[49]

The 1530 ban on icons in the Confucian temple did not extend to other contexts or to other kinds of representation of Confucius, which proliferated in the late Ming and Qing periods. Officials and other members of the educated elite sponsored many variations of an illustrated biography of Confucius, generically known as "Pictures of the Sage's Traces" (*Shengji tu*; see cat. no. 4).[50] The earliest example was an anonymously painted version commissioned in 1444 by the censer Zhang Kai (1398–1460) to illustrate episodes he selected from Sima Qian's biography of Confucius and complemented with his own poetic encomia (*zan*). Circulated through rubbings from the stone tablets he subsequently had carved to preserve the work, Zhang's compilation of pictures and texts inspired a profusion of later versions. These may contain anywhere from a couple dozen to over one hundred scenes, and the events chosen for illustration often reflected the sponsors' priorities.

Late Ming and Qing pictorial biographies of Confucius were made in various media and forms (see cat. nos. 4–5). These include painted handscrolls and albums, woodblock-printed books and portfolios, and incised stone tablets from which rubbings could be taken. Besides appearing in stand-alone form, scenes from the life of Confucius were used to embellish various other kinds of printed text, such as Wu Jiamo's 1589 edition of the *Sayings of the Confucians* (*Kongzi jiayu*) and An Mengsong's 1599 compendium *Complete Writings of the*

Fig. 6. Interior of the Hall of the Sage's Traces (Shengjidian), Temple of Confucius, Qufu, Shandong. Photo: Julia K. Murray

Sage Confucius (*Kongsheng quanshu*).[51] Coinciding with a boom in woodblock publications and a general flourishing of visual culture, the proliferation of pictorial biographies circulated the lively illustrations far and wide. Along with scholars and officials for whom Confucius was a role model, people who did not aspire to serve in government gained opportunities to see and enjoy the pictures,.

In the early 1590s, a set of stone tablets carved with a grand expansion of the pictorial biography was installed in the Hall of the Sage's Traces, which was built explicitly to present the life of Confucius at the Qufu temple (fig. 6).[52] Consisting of 112 pictures inscribed with explanatory accounts and eight tablets of ancillary text, the display was intended as an authoritative interpretation of the sage's actions and teachings. The project was sponsored by a group of high government officials working with the district magistrate of Qufu, Kong Hongfu (active late 16th–early 17th c.), a sixty-first-generation descendant.[53] Two dedicatory inscriptions expressed the donors' hope that seeing Confucius "in action" would inspire viewers to advance in moral cultivation, whether they came in person or saw the pictures only in rubbings. In the early Qing period, a woodblock edition reproducing most of the

Fig. 7. Traditionally attributed to Wu Daozi (ca. 689–after 755), *Bust Portrait of Confucius as Minister of Justice*. Rubbing of a Ming-period stone tablet in the Hall of the Sage's Traces (Shengjidian), Temple of Confucius, Qufu, Shandong. After Édouard Chavannes, *Mission Archéologique dans la Chine Septentrionale*, vol. 6 (Paris, 1909), plate CCCXCVII, no. 870

tablets helped to disseminate the illustrations after the stones themselves became very worn (see cat. no. 5).

Besides the pictorial biography, which occupies the entire north wall of the Hall of the Sage's Traces, several earlier pictorial steles were moved in from other sites around the Qufu temple.[54] Apart from several tablets carved with celebratory calligraphic inscriptions bestowed by the Kangxi and Qianlong emperors, these other stones display portraits of Confucius which purportedly reproduced old paintings transmitted by the Kong lineage. Confucius is depicted in one of several roles and is either alone or accompanied by one or ten disciples. Two of the tablets are uninscribed bust-length representations of Confucius as a minister of justice in Lu (fig. 7), a position he is said to have held for three months in 500 BCE. As in the related painting exhibited here (see cat. no. 1), he is portrayed as a middle-aged figure wearing official robes and a jeweled hat secured with a large pin.[55]

Another portrait stele in the Hall of the Sage's Traces depicts Confucius wearing the same crown-like headgear

Fig. 8. *Confucius and Disciples.* Yuan dynasty, 1242. Woodblock print, from Kong Yuancuo, *Kongshi zuting guangji.* After a facsimile of the exemplar in the National Library of China, Beijing (Rare Book 09594)

but shown full-figure, seated on a dais under a parasol.[56] Ten of his disciples attend him, standing around the sides and back of the platform. An inscription dated to 1095 and signed by Kong Zongshou (active late 11th c.), a forty-sixth-generation descendant, says that the stele reproduced one of two paintings by the famous Tang master Wu Daozi (ca. 689–after 755) that his family owned.[57] Kong Yuancuo later illustrated the composition as a line drawing in his 1242 genealogy, *Kongshi zuting guangji* (fig. 8). Paintings of Confucius among his disciples emphasize his importance as a teacher and mentor, and many were made in later centuries (see cat. nos. 6, 7, and 9).

Kong Zongshou characterized his family's other painting by Wu Daozi, called *Portrait [of Confucius] Practicing the Teaching* (*Xingjiao xiang*), as depicting the standing figures of Confucius and his favorite disciple, Yan Hui. Two of the stone tablets in the Hall of the Sage's Traces reproduce a composition matching this description, although neither bears a title or an artist's name (fig. 9). Dated 1095 and 1118, respectively, they were sponsored by two other members of the Kong lineage, Kong Duanyou and Kong Yu (d. after 1142).[58] Both works show Confucius and the much shorter Yan Hui on a blank background, standing in a dignified pose and facing toward the viewer's left. The two men wear plain robes and clasp their hands in front of their chests. The handle of a sword attached to Confucius's belt protrudes beyond his slightly stooped figure, while Yan Hui's sword is tucked under his arm.

The portrayal of Confucius with Yan Hui also fits the description of a painting known simply as the *Small Portrait* (*Xiao ying*), which was housed in the Kong family shrine (*jiamiao*) during the eleventh century. According to its earliest documentation in a genealogy compiled in 1085, the painting showed Confucius dressed in clothing appropriate for dwelling at leisure, i.e., not official garb. In an updated genealogy published in 1134, Kong Chuan (ca. 1059–ca. 1134) pronounced it "the truest of the Sage's portraits" (*yu Sheng xiang wei zui zhen*), and Kong Yuancuo included a line drawing of it in his 1242 genealogy.[59] The scene was also copied in stone on incised tablets erected at a number of schools in the late Northern Song period.[60] During the late Ming and Qing, several versions of Confucius's pictorial biography used the two-man portrait as a frontispiece illustration, sometimes adding a landscape background. The 112 biographical illustrations incised on stone tablets on the north wall of the Hall of the Sage's Traces begin with this composition.[61]

Three stone tablets along the west wall of the Hall depict Confucius as a solitary standing figure, bending forward slightly and clasping his hands before his chest (e.g., fig. 10). As in his portrayal with Yan Hui, he wears the plain robes and headdress of a private scholar and has a sword tucked under his arm. The three stones differ in size and display slight variations in the details of their shared iconography, suggesting that they may have been carved in different periods. Only one bears a title, date,

Fig. 9. *Confucius and Yan Hui.* Rubbing of Northern Song period stone tablet (dated 1118) sponsored by Kong Yu. Hall of the Sage's Traces (Shengjidian), Temple of Confucius, Qufu, Shandong. Approx. 64 × 40 cm. After Édouard Chavannes, *Mission Archéologique dans la Chine Septentrionale*, vol. 6 (Paris, 1909), plate CCCXCVIII, no. 871

Fig. 10. Traditionally attributed to Wu Daozi (ca. 689–after 755), *Portrait of Confucius.* Rubbing of a Ming-period stone tablet in the Hall of the Sage's Traces (Shengjidian), Temple of Confucius, Qufu, Shandong. H. approx. 195 cm. After Édouard Chavannes, *Mission Archéologique dans la Chine Septentrionale*, vol. 6 [Paris, 1909], plate CCCC, no. 874

and donor inscription, identifying it as the *Small Portrait of the First Teacher* (*Xianshi xiaoxiang*) commissioned in 1735 by the seventieth-generation duke, Kong Guangqi (1713–1743).[62] Equally small is an image paired with Mi Fu's (1051–1107) well-known encomium to Confucius, which is transcribed in bold small-seal script to the right of the figure.[63] Strong contrasts of light and dark bands on Confucius's sashes and hair exemplify a style of carving that was popular in the late Ming and early Qing periods, suggesting a likely date for the stone.

The largest of the three stones (fig. 10) bears a notation at the lower left attributing the portrayal to the Tang artist Wu Daozi, although the carving itself appears to date only

to the late Ming. The figure of Confucius is stockier than in the two smaller stones or in his depictions with Yan Hui, and his voluminous sleeves hang past his knees. With a broad nose and prominent buck teeth, his face is rather homely, and he wears the soft cloth headdress of a recluse. The first four lines of a well-known ode to Confucius are transcribed across the top of the tablet:

His virtue is the equal of heaven and earth,
His Way is the crown of past and present,
He edited and explained the *Six Classics*,
And handed down the statutes for 10,000 ages.

Fig. 11. *Disciples of Confucius.* Contemporary life-size sculptures at the Temple of Confucius, Beijing, with votive placards left by supplicants. Photo: Julia K. Murray

Composed by the eminent academician Chen Fengwu (1475–1541), the text probably dates to around 1519, when Chen participated in a sacrifice at the Qufu temple.[64]

This large untitled portrayal of Confucius closely resembles an image that Kong Duanyou and Kong Chuan had incised on a stele erected at the Quzhou temple in the early Southern Song period. Although the original stone was later destroyed, its iconography was preserved in a mid-Ming replacement that also bears Chen Fengwu's quatrain.[65] The title of the stele, *Legacy Portrait of the First Sage* (*Xiansheng yixiang*), suggests a likeness surviving from Confucius's lifetime. Perhaps the figure was enlarged from the composition showing Confucius attended by Yan Hui, which Kong Duanyou had incised on stone in 1095 and Kong Chuan had described as the most faithful portrait of the Sage.[66] Whatever the origin, large solo representations of Confucius, often bearing attributions to Wu Daozi, circulated widely throughout China in the form of rubbings. These in turn served as models for new stone tablets that were installed at many government schools and private academies, particularly during the Ming and Qing periods.[67] The iconography also inspired many paintings and woodblock-printed book illustrations, and the solo portrait serves as the frontispiece in several pictorial biographies of Confucius.

Recent decades have seen a proliferation of a new kind of image in monumental sculptural representations of Kongzi. Made of stone or metal, they combine the features of the familiar "Wu Daozi" portrayal with the conventions of Western public statuary. The large statues were first erected in Taiwan and and Hong Kong, and then in other parts of the world during the 1970s and 1980s.[68] In the 1990s, the standing figures started to appear in mainland China, initially at Confucian temples that were being restored as tourist attractions, and then on university campuses. The diversity of these images led in 2006 to an official effort to create a standard portrait of Confucius.[69] Most recently, lifesize statues of the disciples and later Confucians based on late Ming woodblock-printed images have also begun to appear (fig. 11).[70]

CONFUCIUS IN THE PRESENT

Confucius historically attracted little interest from the general public until the early twentieth century, when godlike images of him began to be made as colorful woodblock prints for household use (often called "New Year Pictures," or *nianhua*).[71] Now a broad range of people are incorporating Confucius and his disciples into new rituals and practices. Many newly restored temples permit visitors to burn incense at the large outdoor statues of Confucius and before the altars in their main halls, some of which now also display painted or sculptural images. Students anxious about entrance examinations to prestigious schools hang up votive tablets to seek his aid, and supplicants of all ages pray to him for long life, good health, and lots of progeny.

In China and elsewhere, Confucius's teachings are once again being studied for insights on humane self-cultivation and promoted for their applications to contemporary affairs. Since 2004, many "Confucius Institutes" have been set up to teach Chinese language and culture in countries around the world. In 2005, UNESCO established a "Confucius Literacy Prize" to honor individuals working to increase literacy in countries throughout the world, and honorees receive a gold statuette of Confucius along with award funds. As we consider these novel ways of appropriating Confucius in the present, the works in the exhibition remind us of an astute observation made by historian Gu Jiegang (1893–1980): "Each age has its own Confucius, and in any one period there are also various different kinds of Confucius."[72] The ancient sage has played many roles in the past and without a doubt will continue to be a presence in China and the rest of the world.

NOTES

1. Sima Qian, *Shiji*, juan 47, p. 1947.
2. For excellent English-language recent treatments of Confucius's complex persona, see Nylan and Wilson, *The Lives of Confucius*; Wilson, "Ritualizing Confucius / Kongzi"; Csikszentmihalyi, "Confucius"; and Jensen, *Manufacturing Confucianism*.
3. Sima Qian, *Shiji*, juan 47, p. 1947.
4. Sima Qian, *Shiji*, juan 47, pp. 1905–47; Sima Qian, *Selections from Records of the Historian*, pp. 1–27; and Nylan and Wilson, *The Lives of Confucius*, chap. 1.
5. Sima Qian delicately says they were "joined in the wild" (*ye he*) and notes that Confucius's mother would not tell him where his father was buried; *Shiji*, juan 47, pp. 1905–7.
6. Sima Qian, *Shiji*, juan 47, p. 1947.
7. For details, see the fourth-century anthology of stories of anomalous events (*zhiguai*), Wang Jia, *Shiyi ji*, juan 3, pp. 4–5. The anecdotes about Confucius's birth are elaborated in Kong Yuancuo, *Kongshi zuting guangji*, juan 8, pp. 1b–2b.
8. According to correlations in Five Phases theory, the Shang dynasty was associated with water and the Zhou dynasty with wood, which overcomes and thus succeeds water. Because Confucius's ancestors were related to the Shang rulers, his essence was water. Water cannot overcome wood, so Confucius could never become king.
9. E.g., Kong Chuan, *Dongjia zaji*, juan shang, pp. 2a–b (31–32) and juan xia, p. 3b (108), and Kong Yuancuo, *Kongshi zuting guangji*, juan 8, p. 4a (51).
10. Ideas associated with Confucius and his followers are conveniently summarized in *RoutledgeCurzon Encyclopedia of Confucianism*.
11. Wilson argues that Confucius's ideas about gods and spirits have been distorted by modern apologists who presented him as ancient China's "rational humanist"; *Confucian Gods and the Rites to Venerate Them*. For the role of European Jesuit missionaries in molding a conception of Confucius to advance their own agendas, see Jensen, *Manufacturing Confucianism*; also Demattè, "Christ and Confucius."

12. The Five Classics are the *Book of Changes* (*Yijing*), *Book of Poetry* (*Shijing*), *Book of Documents* (*Shujing*), *Book of Rites* (*Liji*), and *Spring and Autumn Annals* (*Chunqiu*); for detailed discussion, see Nylan, *The Five "Confucian" Classics*.
13. The *Four Books* consist of the *Analects*, the *Mencius* (*Mengzi*), and two chapters from the *Book of Rites* (*Liji*): the *Great Learning* (*Daxue*) and *The Constant Mean* (*Zhongyong*); see Gardner, *The Four Books*.
14. Zhu Xi sometimes used kinship terms and rituals to address Confucius as an ancestor; see Tillmann, "Zhu Xi's Prayers to the Spirit of Confucius," pp. 504–5. Sima Qian had portrayed Confucius as the ancestor to ten generations of scholars; *Shiji*, juan 47, p. 1947.
15. *Xinjiaoben Qingshi gao*, juan 7, p. 216, and *Xin Qingshi*, juan 7, p. 492 (both consulted on *Scripta Sinica* [*Hanji dianzi wenjian*], Academia Sinica, Taiwan).
16. For Confucius's changing titles over the centuries, see Wilson, "Ritualizing Confucius / Kongzi," pp. 50–57, or *Da zai Kongzi*, p. 361.
17. For detailed discussions, see Wilson, "Sacrifice and the Imperial Cult of Confucius" and "Ritualizing Confucius / Kongzi."
18. Sima Qian, *Shiji*, juan 47, pp. 1945–6.
19. Wilson, "Ritualizing Confucius / Kongzi," p. 74.
20. For a description of the ritual, see Wilson, "The Ritual Formation of Confucian Orthodoxy," pp. 577–78. A *ding* day was the fourth in a ten-day cycle.
21. For a comprehensive study of the architecture of the Qufu temple, see *Qufu Kongmiao jianzhu*, and for an introduction in English, *Temple and Cemetery of Confucius and the Kong Family Mansion in Qufu*.
22. Although the name "Apricot Terrace" appears in the *Zhuangzi* (*Zhuangzi jishi* "Yufu pian" 31, p. 1023), a stone platform to commemorate it was built only in the eleventh century and a pavilion in the twelfth, with yellow roof tiles added in the eighteenth.
23. Unlike other major buildings on the central axis, which had burned down in the summer of 1724 and were reconstructed on grander scale in Qing palace style with yellow roof tiles, the Hall of the Sage's Traces survived the fire and retained its green Ming-style roof.
24. During periods of political turmoil or dynastic change, conferral of the title was sometimes delayed; for example, see Wilson, "The Ritual Formation of Confucian Orthodoxy," p. 573. In 1935, the title was changed to Sacrificing Official for the Greatly Accomplished Ultimate Sage and First Teacher (*Dacheng zhisheng xianshi fengsiguan*); see Jing, *The Temple of Memories*, p. 39, or *Qufu Kongmiao jianzhu*, p. 444.
25. Before the twentieth century, the Kong Mansion was called the Yanshenggong fu. For detailed information, see Agnew, "Memory and Power in Qufu"; Lamberton, "The Kongs of Qufu"; or *Tianxia diyi jia*.
26. They are reproduced in *Kongzi xiang, Yanshenggong ji furen xiaoxiang*, plates 17–58. From the middle Ming onward, the dukes typically found wives in the families of high court officials; see Agnew, "Culture and Power," pp. 105–6.

27. Kong Yuancuo's preface suggests that he completed his compilation in 1227, but blocks were carved for the publication only in 1242. A section of line-drawn pictures follows the table of contents. For details concerning various Kong genealogies and their agendas, see Agnew, "Memory and Power in Qufu," and Wilson, "The Ritual Formation of Confucian Orthodoxy."

28. Kong Jifen, *Queli wenxian kao, juan* 12, p. 11b (230). All these paintings are reproduced in color in *Kongzi xiang, Yanshenggong ji furen xiaoxiang*, plates 1–12.

29. See Agnew, "Memory and Power in Qufu."

30. See Wilson, "The Ritual Formation of Confucian Orthodoxy," esp. pp. 571–75, and Agnew, "Memory and Power in Qufu."

31. See Hsi-yuan Chen, "Confucianism Encounters Religion."

32. Wang Liang, "The Confucian Temple Tragedy of the Cultural Revolution," and Yazi [Wang Liang], *Kongfu da jienan*. The destruction of 6,618 registered cultural artifacts included 929 paintings, over 2,700 books, 1,000 stone steles, and 2,000 graves; see MacFarquhar and Schoenhals, *Mao's Last Revolution*, p. 119.

33. Wang Liang, "The Confucian Temple Tragedy of the Cultural Revolution," pp. 384–85.

34. See *Pipan Qufu "San Kong."* Because Confucius had an elder brother, calling him "Old Number-Two Kong" was an informal and disrespectful reference to this relationship.

35. The set of 23 pictures was published in October 1974 by the Shanghai People's Press (Shanghai renmin chubanshe); for reproductions and translations, see Kenneth E. Brashier, "Wantonly Distorting the Past," http://people.reed.edu/~brashiek/syllabi/Poster/index.html (accessed October 1, 2009).

36. See Billioud and Thoraval, "*Jiaohua*: The Confucian Revival."

37. For analytical discussion, see Makeham, *Lost Soul*, chap. 5.

38. For numerous images, see Luo Chenglie, *Huaxiang zhong de Kongzi*; Wang Shucun, *Kongzi baitu*; Kaji Nobuyuki, *Kōshi gaden*; and Laufer, "Confucius and His Portraits." I have written extensively about various categories of visual representation; see Murray, "'Idols' in the Temple," "Varied Views of the Sage," "Portraits of Confucius," "Illustrations of the Life of Confucius," "The Temple of Confucius and Pictorial Biographies of the Sage," and "The Hangzhou *Portraits of Confucius and Seventy-two Disciples (Sheng xian tu)."*

39. Ban Gu, *Hanshu, juan* 30, p. 1717. Art historians have suggested that the work was a copybook for artisans; see Wu Hung, "The Earliest Pictorial Representations of Ape Tales," p. 91, and Powers, "Pictorial Art and its Public," p. 141. A scholar of early Chinese thought translates the title as "Charts and Models of Confucius and His Disciples" and speculates that the work contained encoded prophecies rather than portraits; see Csikszentmihalyi, "Confucius and the *Analects* in the Han," p. 142.

40. Fan Ye, *Hou Hanshu, juan* 60 *xia*, p. 1998, biography of Cai Yong. Handscrolls preserving small-scale replicas of these portraits were still extant in the late Tang; see Zhang Yanyuan, *Lidai minghua ji, juan* 3, p. 54.

41. This connection is made in 1563 by Sun Ying'ao, the Shaanxi inspector of education, in his inscription for a portrait stele at the Xi'an Prefectural School; see the rubbing reproduced in *Beijing tushuguan cang huaxiang taben huibian*, vol. 1, p. 107. However, a careful review of the documentary evidence strongly suggests that the images were added in the late second century, nearly four centuries after Wen Weng's time; see Farmer, "Art, Education, and Power."

42. See reproductions in Luo Chenglie, *Huaxiang zhong de Kongzi*, plates 2–15; also *Zhongguo huaxiang shi quanji*, vol. 2, plates 97, 99, 101, 131 & 139. Several are reproduced and analyzed in Powers, *Art and Political Expression in Early China*. A few examples from Jiaxiang have been attributed to the first century BCE; see Erickson, "*Que* Pillars at the Wu Family Cemetery," pp. 120–26.

43. Sima Qian, *Shiji, juan* 47, p. 1909, and *juan* 63, p. 2140. Later, Han emperor Huandi (r. 147–67) built a temple to Laozi and had a portrait of Confucius painted on the wall (suggesting that he was subordinate to Laozi), and descendant Kong Chou set up a stele to Confucius in front of it; see Chen Shou, *Sanguo zhi Wei shu, juan* 16, pp. 514–15.

44. Sima Qian, *Shiji, juan* 71, p. 2319, and *Huainanzi, juan* 19, p. 208. For detailed analysis, see Soymié, "L'entrevue de Confucius et de Hiang T'o."

45. For detailed discussion and references, see Murray, "'Idols' in the Temple"; see also Sommer, "Destroying Confucius."

46. Li Daoyuan, *Shuijing zhu, juan* 25, entry for the River Si (Sishui), and Kong Yuancuo, *Kongshi zuting guangji, juan* 10, pp. 8a–11b, text of Li Yan (or Ting) stele, dated 541. Both are quoted and discussed in *Qufu Kongmiao jianzhu*, p. 54.

47. See Sommer, "Images into Words" and "Destroying Confucius."

48. Huang Jinxing, "Kongmiao de jiegou yu chongzu," pp. 128–29.

49. The current sculpture replaced one that was destroyed by Red Guards in 1966 during the Cultural Revolution. The earlier icon had been made by artisans sent from Beijing by the Yongzheng emperor (r. 1723–35) to help restore the Qufu temple after a disastrous fire in 1724; see Kong Jifen, *Queli wenxian kao, juan* 12, pp. 10a–b (222–28), and *Xichao xinyu, juan* 9, p. 1b (336).

50. For detailed discussions, see Murray, "Illustrations of the Life of Confucius," "The Temple of Confucius and Pictorial Biographies of the Sage," and "Varied Views of the Sage."

51. Wu Jiamo (*jinshi* 1607) engaged noted artists and block-carvers to copy pictures from a now-unknown edition that his teacher brought from Qufu to Hangzhou and added them to his reproduction of a Song edition of *Kongzi jiayu*. The resulting *Kongsheng jiayu tu* was immediately pirated by commercial publishers. A convenient modern reproduction appears in *Zhongguo gudai banhua congkan, er bian*, vol. 3, pp. 1–550. An Mengsong excerpted several of Wu Jiamo's illustrations to enhance *Kongsheng quanshu*, a handbook of assorted Confucian writings that Zheng Yunzhu (a.k.a. Zheng Shihao) of the Zongwen shushe published commercially. For further discussion and references, see Murray, "Varied Views of the Sage," p. 239.

52. I discuss the creation and history of this set in detail in Murray, "The Temple of Confucius and Pictorial Biographies of the Sage" and "Varied Views of the Sage," pp. 243–47.

53. Kong Hongfu's participation in the Shengjidian project suggests ideas about governance somewhat different from those of the Kong duke. Although the duke had the hereditary right to appoint the magistrate, he sometimes had to make concessions to other branches of Kongs who allied themselves with local gentry to gain greater influence in local affairs; see Agnew, "Culture and Power," chap. 2. A later administrative gazetteer comments that when Kong Hongfu took office, he found preparations against natural disasters such as flood or drought completely lacking, so he set up twenty-four granaries, implying that the duke had been remiss; *Qufu xian zhi*, juan 91, pp. 3a–b (2085–86).

54. The stones in the Shengjidian are itemized in Kong Jifen, *Queli wenxian kao*, juan 12, p. 3a (213). For a more detailed account, illustrated with rubbings, see Baba Harukichi, *Kōshi seiseki shi*, pp. 159–74.

55. Reproduced in Luo Chenglie, *Huaxiang zhong de Kongzi*, plate 16, and Baba Harukichi, *Kōshi seiseki shi*, p. 164.

56. Reproduced in Luo Chenglie, *Huaxiang zhong de Kongzi*, plate 23, and Baba Harukichi, *Kōshi seiseki shi*, p. 166.

57. These attributions were probably optimistic, as portrayals of Confucius are not mentioned in Wu Daozi's biography in Zhang Yanyuan's *Lidai minghua ji*, juan 9, pp. 108–9. I discuss Wu Daozi's connection with portraits of Confucius in greater detail in Murray, "Pedagogue on the Go" (forthcoming).

58. Kong Duanyou became the 48th-generation Duke for Perpetuating the Sage in 1104; Kong Yu was a 49th-generation descendant who remained in Qufu after the 1126/27 Jin conquest. The two steles are reproduced in Luo Chenglie, *Huaxiang zhong de Kongzi*, plates 17 and 21, and Baba Harukichi, *Kōshi seiseki shi*, pp. 168 and 165. Starting in the Yuan period, Kong family publications sometimes ascribed the portrayal to Gu Kaizhi (ca. 345–ca. 406), an attribution now associated with the stele on the north wall of the Hall of the Sage's Traces. I review the origins and credibility of this attribution in Murray, "Pedagogue on the Go."

59. The 1085 genealogy was compiled by Kong Zonghan (active 11th c.), a member of the 46th generation of the senior Kong lineage. His text does not survive independently but was subsumed into later editions. For the description of the *Small Portrait*, see Kong Chuan, *Dongjia zaji, juan xia*, pp. 3b–4a (108–9), and Kong Yuancuo, *Kongshi zuting guangji*, juan 8, p. 3b (51). The line drawing appears in Kong Yuancuo's book as the first plate following the table of contents and is given the title *Small Portrait [of Confucius with] Master Yan Following (Xiao ying, Yanzi congxing)*.

60. I discuss school tablets in greater detail in Murray, "Pedagogue on the Go." A rubbing of the stele carved in 1124 for the school in Shaoxing is reproduced in *Beijing tushuguan cang huaxiang taben huibian*, vol. 1, p. 4.

61. See reproduction in Luo Chenglie, *Huaxiang zhong de Kongzi*, plate 22.

62. Reproduced in Baba Harukichi, *Kōshi seiseki shi*, p. 164. The carver is also identified—one Zhu Chengrui of Piling.

63. Reproduced in Baba Harukichi, *Kōshi seiseki shi*, p. 163. A copy of this stone was made in 1821 for the (now-destroyed) temple of Confucius on Mount Tai (Taishan); see the rubbing reproduced in Zhang Qiyun, *Kong Meng shengji tushuo*, p. 2.

64. A stone tablet set in the walls of a stele pavilion at the Qufu temple preserves Chen Fengwu's account of his visit and sacrifice in 1519. The full text of his "Encomium to the First Sage and King of Propagating Culture" (*Xiansheng wenxuanwang zan*) appears on an adjacent tablet carved under the sponsorship of Qufu magistrate Kong Gongtong, who held that office from 1516 to 1522; see *Qufu xian zhi*, juan 39, pp. 14b–15a (1118–19). Chen Fengwu, a native of Luling (Jiangxi) and a 1496 *jinshi*, was also known for his patronage of the Yuelu Academy in Jiangling (modern Changsha, Hunan).

65. Reproduced in Murray, "'Idols' in the Temple," p. 398, fig. 9; Luo Chenglie, *Huaxiang zhong de Kongzi*, plate 27; and *Qufu Kongmiao jianzhu*, p. 3, fig. 1-1-2. I speculate about its origins at greater length in Murray, "Pedagogue on the Go."

66. Even if Kong Duanyou and Kong Chuan did not bring a rubbing with them from Qufu, incised tablets depicting Confucius with Yan Hui were readily available at schools, such as one installed in 1124 in relatively nearby Shaoxing (Zhejiang); reproduced in *Beijing tushuguan cang huaxiang taben huibian*, vol. 1, p. 4.

67. For rubbings of examples dating from 1440 to 1721, see *Beijing tushuguan cang huaxiang taben huibian*, vol. 1, plates 97, 102, 132 & 174.

68. In 1974, at the height of the "Criticize Confucius, Criticize Lin Biao" campaign on the mainland, the Nationalist government in Taiwan promoted its own commitment to China's ancient heritage by disseminating images of Confucius. The "Wu Daozi" portrait was identified as the most reliable model by Kong Decheng (1920–2008), who had grown up in Qufu and was the 77th-generation duke; further discussed in Murray, "The Global Rebranding of Confucius."

69. For a detailed account, see Murray, "The Global Rebranding of Confucius."

70. Their iconography is based on the images in Lü Weiqi's *Shengxian xiangzan*. Lü's portrayals copied a set of Southern Song incised tablets in Hangzhou; for rubbings see *Beijing tushuguan cang huaxiang taben huibian*, vol. 1, plates 6–76; for critical analysis, see Murray, "The Hangzhou *Portraits of Confucius and Seventy-two Disciples (Sheng xian tu)*."

71. Several are reproduced in Wang Shucun, *Kongzi baitu*, pp. 15–20.

72. For slightly different translations and discussions of Gu's statement, see Wilson, "Ritualizing Confucius / Kongzi," p. 87, and Csikszentmihalyi, "Confucius and the *Analects* in the Han," p. 153.

种种不同的孔子：师者，政客，圣人

如果有一个人可以在世界范围内代表中华文明，那么这个人应当是孔子(公元前551-公元前479年)：伟大的思想家，教育家和道德家。虽然孔子卒于约2500年前，但在其身后漫长的岁月里，他一直被尊崇为文圣。孔子传道授业，其本人的德行与政事也垂范后世。他的一生是个人品行道德的典范，而其为政的学说，则为中国长达两千余年的王朝统治提供了善政理论。其影响甚而波及东南亚邻国，于今绵延不绝。

孔子出生于周公封地的小邦鲁国（今山东曲阜），家贫早孤，但他年少时即仰慕周公制礼作乐，建立章程。遂有学于此，志在恢复。中年时，孔子周游北部列国，游说诸侯，希望寻求一位理想的君主来施行仁政，恢复礼乐和先贤之道，然而他的努力却收效甚微。十四年后，他重返鲁国。此后，孔子专心教育，广收门徒，有弟子三千，贤人七十二，并开始编定整理后来所说的"经"，也就是中国精英教育的核心读本。

孔子七十三岁寿终正寝。他最亲近的弟子以父丧之礼为他守孝三年。孔子故居被改作庙宇，即今山东曲阜孔庙的雏形。孔子后人及其门人弟子和后世学者，继承发展了他的思想，将他与弟子、君王等人的对话，鲜活地保存在《论语》一书中；汉太史司马迁为孔子撰写了编年传记。汉代及后世帝王多追谥孔子，并支持曲阜祭孔。唐代时，孔子被奉为"文宣王"至明嘉靖九年则改为"至圣先师"。京师及各地官学都建有孔庙，每年春秋祭祀孔子、孔子弟子及后世贤人。一直到清代晚期，祭祀者、祭器、音乐等的数量和种类都由政府提供和调配。民国时期，虽祭祀仪式有所变化，规模也有所缩减，但祭孔的活动仍在继续。

曲阜孔庙因享有历朝历代的供给而一再扩大，愈见显赫。到十八世纪，曲阜孔庙形成了在三条南北向轴线上延伸的建筑群，并有高墙环绕，与外界分隔，其规模堪比宫殿。孔庙中最宏伟的建筑是拥有巨大重檐，红墙黄瓦的大成殿。大成殿由雕有云龙高浮雕的石柱分割成九间。作为孔庙的祭祀正殿，大成殿供奉有孔子，四配（颜回，曾子，子思，孟子）以及十二哲（十一弟子和朱熹）的雕像和祭坛。另一处重要的建筑是绿檐的圣迹殿，内中陈列着孔子像石碑和《圣迹图》。《圣迹图》由112个场景组成，以图像的形式展现了孔子生平和后代祭孔发展中的重大事件。在十三御碑亭内外，许多石碑刻有颂扬孔子的题赞，这些文字多出于亲临曲阜献祭的历代君王之手。有些碑文则记录了孔庙在各阶段的重大修缮和重建的历史。造访孔庙最频繁的君王是清代的乾隆皇帝，他的八临孔庙既是出于他个人对孔子的敬仰，也有他欲借重孔子的圣名来巩固清王朝统治的考虑。

历朝历代还给与孔子后裔世袭爵位及物质利益。孔子后裔享有免税权，世袭官位和田地。田地的出产物用以负担常规的家祭费用和孔氏家族日常费用。从1055年到1935年，袭爵为衍圣公的孔氏嫡孙都居住在孔庙附近恢宏的宅子里。明代中期以后保存下来的诸衍圣公及夫人的肖像，昭示出他们的尊荣地位。为了制衡孔子后裔对其特权的使用，孔氏一族制作了详细的族谱和皇室馈赠记录。他们出版的文献中还包含了家传孔子传说，孔庙的规制和陈设，重要碑文，以及祭器全谱和孔府保存的孔子图像等。

孔子的图像是在其辞世后很久才出现的。现存最早的孔子像只能追溯到公元一世纪。孔子的图像是多种多样的。可见在对孔子重要性的认识上，存在着不同的观点。我们可以从明代中期起开始出现的画本、木刻本和石刻本等不同版本的《圣迹图》中清楚地看到这一点。在单独描绘孔子的图象中，常常可以看到一个身著朝服的孔子。不过，素净长袍的装扮则更为常见，展现了孔子作为教师和学者的一面。孔庙中的孔子塑像则是帝王的装束，更像道教和民间祭神中的主神。1530年，嘉靖皇帝禁止各官学的文庙供奉孔子像。此后各地文庙改为供奉孔子和弟子和后世贤人的牌位，而帝王形象的孔子塑像就只存留于曲阜孔庙和孔氏家庙中了。

但是禁令并没未影响其他形象的孔子像。事实上在明清之际，孔子像曾大量出现于中国各地官学和书院内的石碑上，并屡见于绘画和木刻本书籍中，在这些肖像中，孔子被奉为师者和学者和官仕的楷模。一本11世纪的孔氏族谱中选择了最常见的这样两种孔子像的构图，一种是孔子的单人立像，另一种则有孔子最喜爱的弟子颜回侍立一旁。这两种图像的拓片被不断地重刻到新石碑上，有时还可见"唐吴道子画"的款识。

近几十年来一种新的孔子图像--孔子大雕像--大量出现。这些雕像多为石质或金属材质，融合了广为人知的所谓"吴道子画孔子像"的要素和西方公共大雕塑的常规手法。这种大雕像最初于1974年出现在台湾。二十世纪七十年代到八十年代见于世界其他地区。到二十世纪九十年代，中国大陆逐渐开始出现这种立像。在中国大陆，这些立像最早被放置在重建为观光胜地的各处文庙中，后来则扩展到大学校园内。最近还出现了真人大小的孔子弟子及后代贤人像，并逐渐成为新的民间祭祀仪式的焦点。如今的祭孔者多为焦虑的考生和祈求健康长寿、多子多孙的普通百姓。

在中国和世界的其他地区，孔子学说的当代应用引起了人们的关注，因此，孔子的图像也被用于各种目的。这次展览可谓正当其时。展览中的许多作品会让人们想起历史学家顾颉刚的一个论述，"各时代有各时代的孔子，即在一个时代中也有种种不同的孔子呢"。孔子已经在历史中扮演了许多角色，毋庸置疑，他还将继续存在于当今中国乃至于世界的现实中。

孟久丽　编写
邹　昕　翻译

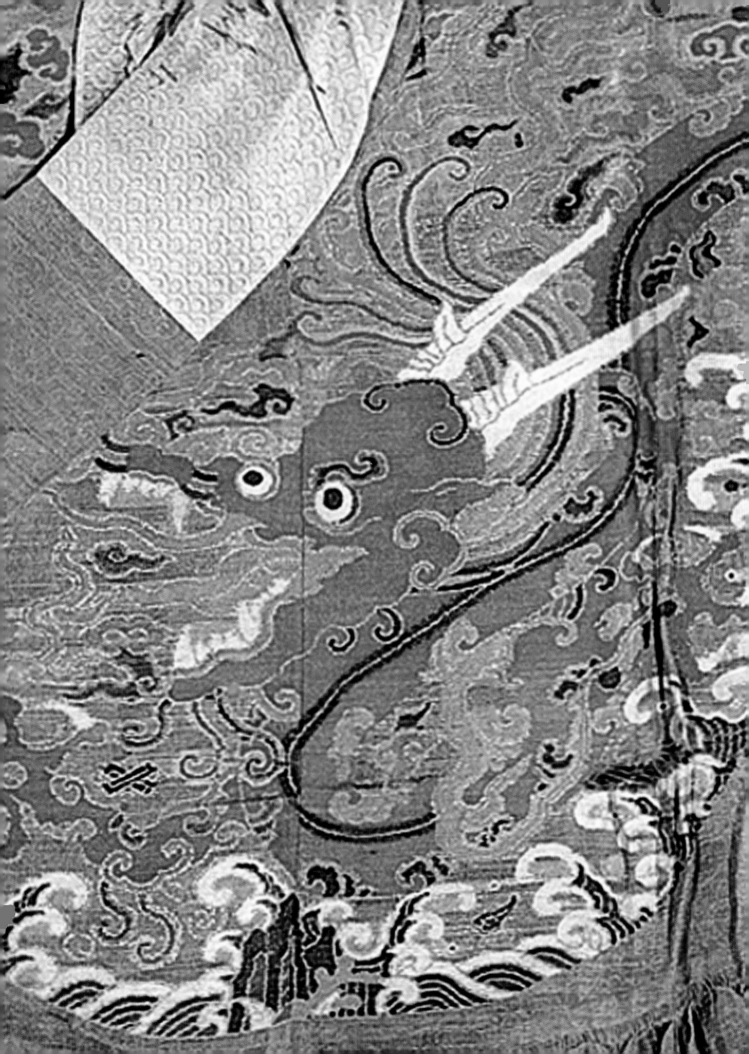

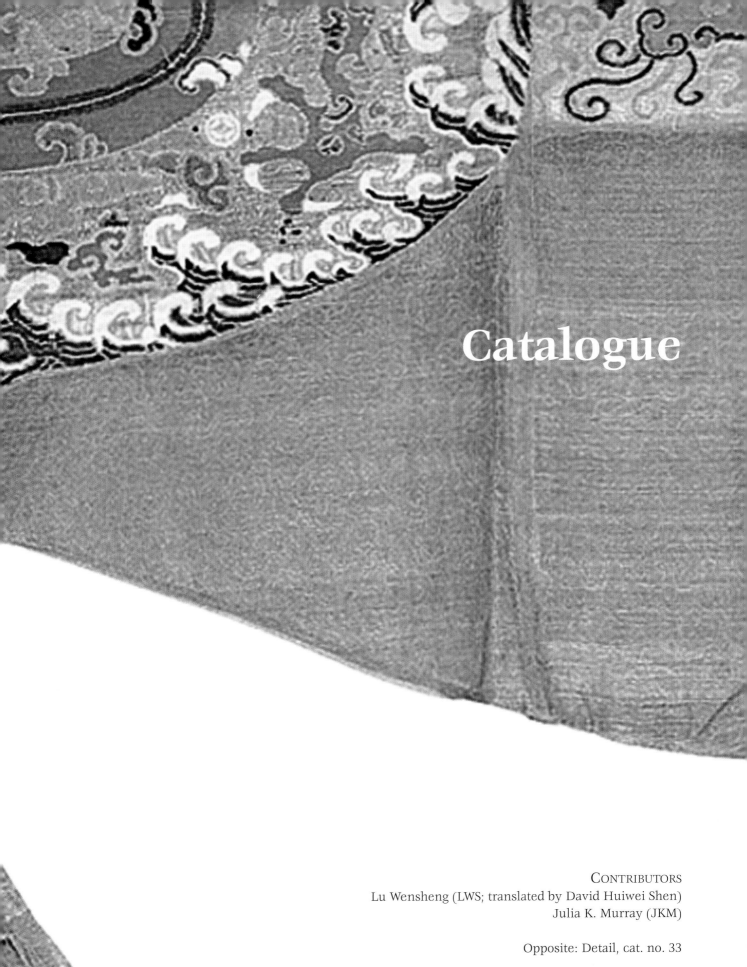

Catalogue

CONTRIBUTORS
Lu Wensheng (LWS; translated by David Huiwei Shen)
Julia K. Murray (JKM)

Opposite: Detail, cat. no. 33

1

Anonymous

Portrait of Confucius as Minister of Justice in Lu
明代　孔子为司寇像　立轴
Ming dynasty (1368–1644)
Hanging scroll; ink and color on paper
117.5 × 65.7 cm (painting only)
147.7 × 77.3 cm (painting and colophons)
273.5 × 91.5 cm (overall with mounting)
Shandong Provincial Museum

COLOPHONS

(Above painting) Zhu Shenzao 朱神凿 (1450–1493, Prince Hui of Shu [Shu Hui wang 蜀惠王]);[1] eight-line poetic eulogy titled "Portrait of Greatly Accomplished Confucius When He Was Lu Minister of Justice" (*Dacheng Kongzi wei Lu sikou shi xiang* 大成孔子为鲁司寇时像), dated "on a solstice in [1485]" (*Chenghua yisi sui zhiri* 成化乙巳岁至日) and signed "Reverently eulogized by the Prince of Shu" (*Shuwang jin zan* 蜀王谨赞). Large regular-script calligraphy on floral-patterned silk damask:

元气萃聚，圣智生成，天地之度，日月之明，帝王模范，古今准程，德尊万代，道著六经.

(Left of painting) Kong Xianyi 孔宪彝 (*juren*, 1837; 72nd-generation descendant of Confucius);[2] dated in correspondence with November 2, 1862 (Tongzhi 1/9/11). Small regular script on paper, separately mounted:

On the *dingchou* day of the eighth month of the *renxu* year of Tongzhi [September 20, 1862], before the birthday of the Sage, Wuchang prefect Rushan [ca. 1815–after 1885][3] respectfully installed [this] portrait of the Sage at the Shandong Sojourners' Lodge [Jiangzuo huiguan, in Beijing] to perform a sacrifice.[4] Descendants [Kong] Xianyi, Xiangeng, Xiangu, Qingdu, Qinglu, and Qingce all participated as deacons.[5] The following month, the 74th-generation Duke for Perpetuating the Sage, [Kong] Fanhao [1806–1862; acceded 1841], came to Beijing for an audience [with the emperor]. When he went back, he took [the painting] to return to [its proper place in?] Queli [Qufu] and carefully and reverently stored it in the temple. Respectfully inscribed by [Kong] Xianyi, reader-in-waiting at the Grand Secretariat [*neige shidu*], on the eleventh day of the ninth month of the *renxu* year of the Tongzhi reign [November 2, 1862].[6]

同治元年秋八月丁丑，圣诞前武昌知府如山恭奉圣像至山左会馆致祭，裔孙宪彝、宪庚、宪毂、庆笃、庆篆、庆策皆执事，越月七十四代孙衍圣公繁灏展观来京，因奉归阙里，敬谨藏于庙。壬戌九月十一日内阁侍读，宪彝谨识.

Portraits of Confucius through the centuries have depicted him in a great variety of roles, reflecting both the fluctuations in his social position in life and the posthumous honors awarded to him after his death. Here he wears the clothing and headgear of a high-ranking official, a reference to his brief service as minister of justice in his home state of Lu. During the three months of his administration, order and harmony prevailed throughout the realm.[7] His facial expression in this painting suggests the conscientious attention he devoted to his responsibilities. Appropriate for a man in his mid-fifties, he has a dark moustache and a fine, full beard that hangs in long wavy wisps.

Although portrayals of Confucius as a teacher wearing plain robes and cap became the norm after 1530, when the Jiajing emperor (r. 1522–66) designated him Ultimate Sage and First Teacher (*Zhisheng xianshi*), alternative depictions of Confucius as a high official have a compelling pedigree. Starting in the eleventh century, Kong descendants repeatedly claimed that the famous Tang painter Wu Daozi

(ca. 689–after 755) had painted a portrait of Confucius as minister of justice.[8] In the 1552 update of the *Gazetteer of Queli* (*Queli zhi*; see cat. no. 3), a line-drawing of a bust-length painting labeled *Lu sikou xiang* replaced the full-length figure holding a tablet that had appeared in the original 1505 edition. Besides bearing the same title, both versions of the portrait are annotated with the same information about the colors in the original painting.[9] The substitution suggests that the Ming prince's 1485 endorsement had given the bust portrait greater credibility.[10] A mid-eighteenth-century inventory of paintings of Confucius in the Kong Mansion lists three paintings associated with Wu Daozi: a work on paper, titled *Sikou xiang*, attributed to Wu himself; a copy of Wu's *Sikou xiang*, also on paper, made by Ming Prince Hui of Shu; and an anonymous Song copy on silk, on which the Wanli emperor (r. 1572–1620) had transcribed Song Gaozong's encomium to Confucius.[11] The latter two are extant.

Images of Confucius as minister of justice may have appealed particularly to officials, for whom he was the ultimate role-model. Two incised stone tablets preserving the "Wu Daozi" bust-portrait composition (see p. 21, fig. 7) are displayed in the Qufu temple's Hall of the Sage's Traces (Shengjidian), which was built on the initiative of officials and intended as a place where they could "see" Confucius.[12] A line-drawing of the image illustrates the entry on Confucius in *Sancai tuhui*, the encyclopedia compiled by a retired late-Ming official who also published extensively on problems of public administration.[13]

Compared with these other versions, the Shandong Provincial Museum's *Portrait of Confucius as Minister of Justice* displays greater attention to the details of Confucius's costume. The base of his five-crested crown is a gold-bordered red band, ornamented with cloud-shaped gold fittings and a green jewel set in a circle of pearls.[14] The black upper part is secured with a green hairpin that pierces a gold and pearl eyelet. His blue capstrings have gold grommets at the top and red beads on the tassels hanging from the bow tied under his chin. Finely drawn white flower-and-tendril designs adorn his inner robe, which lies loosely around his neck. He wears a grey outer robe covered with a pattern of auspicious motifs—bats, dragons, scrolling clouds, and flaming jewels—which is depicted in a continuous manner under angular and arbitrarily superimposed fold-lines.

The depiction of Confucius with heavy-lidded eyes and an intense, almost brooding expression, also distinguishes this portrait from others of similar composition. Moreover, he appears to have buck teeth, an attribute also seen in some full-length representations of Confucius as a lone standing figure (see p. 23, fig. 10). This feature seems to have originated with a copyist's misunderstanding of an image of Confucius with his mouth open to speak. Later, the mistake became widespread through replication: probably when rubbings from school steles incorporating it were used for making new stones and as models for paintings.

Although Prince Hui of Shu's encomium is mounted above this portrait, Kong Xianyi's note indicates that the painting went to Qufu only after 1862, so it is not the work recorded in the Kong Mansion in 1762.[15] Moreover, Kong Xianyi does not mention the prince's poem, which is prominently transcribed on a pristine piece of patterned silk damask. Prince Hui's version is probably to be identified with a much more battered painting, still extant in Qufu, which has virtually the same composition and the prince's text written inside the pictorial space. Because the two portraits are so similar, the prince's encomium was probably copied to embellish the newly acquired painting.[16]

JKM

1. Descended from the eleventh son of the Ming founder, Zhu Shenzao was the seventh-generation Prince of Shu, posthumously titled Hui, whose principality was in Chengdu (Sichuan); for his epitaph and gravesite, see *Min'guo Huayang xian zhi*, juan 31, pp. 81a–83a (527–28). The pristine condition of the colophon silk and absence of seals after the signature suggest a later transcription of the prince's text, as discussed at the end of this entry.

2. Kong Xianyi (*zi*, Xuzhong; *hao*, Xiushan) achieved the provincial *juren* degree in 1837 and was a secretary in the Beijing Secretariat (*Neige*). He was an accomplished calligrapher and painter and published several collections of poetry, including *Duiyuelou shi xulu*, *Hanzhai wengao*, *Qufu shichao*, and *Queli Kongshi shichao*; see *Qing huajia shishi*, juan geng xia [14], p. 077-162.

3. A Manchu of the Bordered Blue Banner, Rushan was a 1838 *jinshi*, served as an official in Sichuan and Zhejiang, and was a noted calligrapher and painter; see his brief biography in Yu Jianhua, *Zhongguo meishujia renming cidian*, p. 190. It is not clear where he obtained the painting of Confucius.

4. Native-place lodges in Beijing were institutions that provided short- or long-term lodgings and catered to the social and professional needs of elite men from the same region sojourning in the capital. Altars to local deities and famous men were often maintained there, so a portrait of Confucius was appropriate to bring to Shandong's lodge. For detailed discussions, see Belsky, *Localities at the Center*, chap. 3.

5. The three men with "Xian" in their names (the first one is the colophon's author) belong to the seventy-second generation of descendants; those with "Qing" to the seventy-third. A list of temple offices and hereditary positions controlled by the duke in the Qing period shows that some forty descendants held the salaried position of deacon (*zhishi*) at the Qufu temple, essentially a sinecure with nominal duties related to sacrificial preparations; see *Tianxia diyi jia*, p. 227.

6. Duke Kong Fanhao died on November 11, just over a week after Kong Xianyi wrote this colophon.

7. Sima Qian, *Shiji*, juan 47, p. 1917. See also the illustration of scene 15 in the *Shengji tu* album of paintings (cat. no. 4).

8. I discuss these references in Murray, "Pedagogue on the Go" (forthcoming).

9. No information on provenance accompanies the "minister of justice" portrait in either the 1505 or 1552 edition of *Queli zhi*, in contrast to the other three images of Confucius reproduced from pictures in Kong Yuancuo's *Kongshi zuting guangji* (1242), which in turn allegedly reproduced paintings in the Kongs' possession.

10. However, later editions of *Queli zhi* and the related *Queli guangzhi* reverted back to the full-length version, in which Confucius holds an official's tablet.

11. Kong Jifen, *Queli wenxian kao*, juan 12, p. 11b (230). The allegedly original "Wu Daozi" painting on paper has disappeared. The other two survive and have been published as anonymous Ming works; see *Kongzi xiang, Yanshenggong ji furen xiaoxiang*, plates 8 and 4, respectively. Song Gaozong composed his often-quoted encomium to Confucius (and separate encomia for each of the seventy-two disciples) to accompany the set of pictures he had incised on stone tablets in 1156 for installation in the newly reestablished imperial university in the Southern Song "temporary capital" at Hangzhou; see Murray, "The Hangzhou Portraits of Confucius and Seventy-two Disciples."

12. See the discussion of the Shengjidian in my catalogue essay, pp. 21–23. The titles of the stones are recorded in Kong Jifen, *Queli wenxian kao*, juan 12, p. 3a (213); also Baba Harukichi, *Kōshi seiseki shi*, pp. 159–74.

13. Wang Qi, *Sancai tuhui*, renwu juan 4, p. 17b (626). The illustration is titled "Portrait of the First Sage" (*Xiansheng xiang*), suggesting that Wang Qi regarded it as the standard one. The following page reproduces a second bust portrait, titled "Alternative Portrait of the First Sage" (*Xiansheng bie xiang*), which depicts Confucius in plain clothing; ibid., p. 18a (626).

14. The application of tiny dots of white on the jewels to suggest reflections of light is a technique thought not to predate the Qing, raising a question about the actual date of execution.

15. See note 11.

16. Reproduced in *Kongzi xiang, Yanshenggong ji furen xiaoxiang*, plate 8.

2

Pair of statues of Confucius and his wife, Madame Qiguan

宋代　孔子和亓官夫人楷木像

Song dynasty (960–1279)
Wood, originally painted
Confucius: H. 37 cm, W. 15.5 cm
Madame Qiguan: H. 42 cm, W. 16 cm
The Confucius Museum in Qufu, Shandong Province

Formerly housed at the "Southern Kong" temple in Quzhou, Zhejiang, these simple but evocative wooden figures represent votive images of Confucius and his wife. According to traditional accounts, the forty-eighth-generation duke, Kong Duanyou (d. 1132), brought them from Qufu while fleeing from the invading Jurchen Jin army in the late 1120s.[1] Later, they were installed at the Quzhou temple in a building called Pavilion for Thinking of Lu (Si Lu ge), referring to Qufu.

Carved in the round, Confucius and his wife are depicted as heavily-robed seated figures with disproportionately large heads and expressive eyes. Wearing an official headdress, Confucius has a long, tapering beard and slender hands clasped in front of his chest. Madame Qiguan's hair is gathered into a topknot, and her hands are hidden within her joined sleeves. The wood surfaces display the remains of painted detail and bits of textile, perhaps from an old repair.

Longstanding tradition has it that the effigies were carved by the disciple Zigong, who stayed at Confucius's grave for six years, twice as long as the other disciples. There he planted a pistache tree (kaimu), also known as the "scholar's tree," which was native to his home in the south.[2] The figurines are made from this kind of wood.[3]

The creation of wooden effigies for use in a funerary context represents an ancient and enduring tradition in China, and many examples have been found in early Han tombs. The famous story of the filial son Ding Lan, which is sometimes illustrated on Han funerary shrines, centers on wooden images he carved as surrogates for his deceased parents. Nonetheless, recent scholarship suggests that the figurines of Confucius and his wife are more likely to have been made during the Song period.[4] It seems possible that they were created in the twelfth century to enhance the legitimacy of the Southern Kong dukes. Not long after Kong Duanyou went south and received the patronage of the Southern Song emperor Gaozong, the Jin regime in the north installed his younger brother as duke in Qufu. Competing lines of dukes continued until the Mongols reunified the country under the Yuan dynasty.

JKM

1. *Min'guo Quxian zhi*, juan 3, p. 16b (692).
2. A fossilized stump near Confucius's grave in Qufu is identified today as the remains of the tree planted by Zigong; see *Qufu: Kongzi de guxiang*, p. 121, or *Tianxia diyi jia*, p. 109, plate 182. A Ming stele commemorates the site of his hut, which has been rebuilt several times in recent centuries; see *Temple and Cemetery of Confucius and the Kong Family Mansion in Qufu*, p. 71.
3. In 1930, having seen the figures several times, Yu Shaosong reported that the wood had fossilized, which seems not to be the case, and that the antique simplicity of the carving convinced him of their pre-Han date, whether or not they had been carved by Zigong; see Zhang Qiyun, *Kong Meng shengji tushuo*, p. 6, fig. 6.
4. See Luo Chenglie, *Huaxiang zhong de Kongzi*, notes to plate 37.

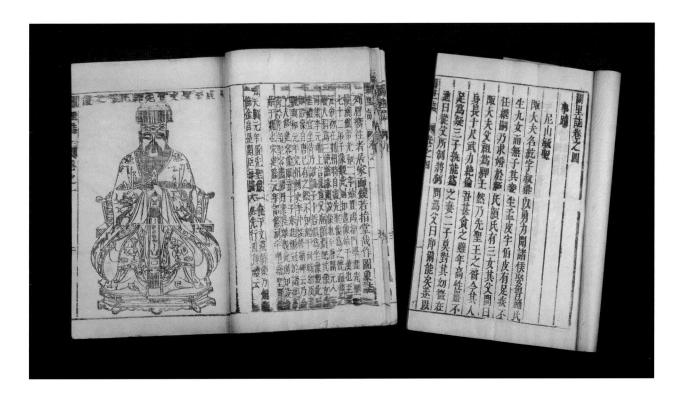

3
Queli zhi (Gazetteer of Queli [Qufu])
明代　陈镐撰, 孔胤植补（清雍正补修）《阙里志》
Qing dynasty, Yongzheng period (1723–35)
Woodblock-printed book
H. 24.4 cm, W. 16.9 cm (closed),
　　　W. 29 cm (open), D. 11 cm
The Confucius Museum in Qufu, Shandong Province

After a major fire in 1499 destroyed the temple of
Confucius in Qufu, the Ming Hongzhi emperor (r. 1487–
1505) sponsored its reconstruction and expansion into a
much grander facility than ever before. Upon its
completion five years later, he sent Grand Secretary and
Minister of Rites Li Dongyang (1447–1516) to perform a
sacrifice there on his behalf.[1] During his stay, Li
instructed the provincial vice-commissioner of education,
Chen Gao (*jinshi*, 1487), to compile an official gazetteer to
supplement existing publications, such as Kong
genealogies, which treated only certain aspects of the
area's history.[2] Rather than recording just the kinds of
administrative information typical of a local gazetteer,
however, Chen Gao organized his *Queli zhi* around
Confucius's significance to the Qufu region.

Completed in 1505 and prefaced with a long
commemorative text by Li Dongyang, the gazetteer drew
together material from a variety of sources, including

earlier publications by Kong descendants, stele
inscriptions in the temple and cemetery, and documents
in the imperial secretariat. In addition, the book contains
far more illustrations than an ordinary gazetteer. Besides
the customary map of the locality, the front section
reproduces, as line-drawings, portraits of Confucius and
plans of the temple, cemetery, and other significant sites.
The section on ritual and music provides diagrams of
altar layouts, pictures of vessels and musical instruments
used during the sacrifice, and stop-motion illustrations of
ceremonial dance choreography. The text includes a
detailed genealogy and successive titles of Confucius and
his senior line of descendants; biographies and titles of
his disciples; transcriptions of imperial awards, edicts,
and stele inscriptions; liturgical texts and eulogies; tomb
epitaphs; and so forth.

Chen Gao's 1505 edition of *Queli zhi*, organized into
thirteen *juan*, was updated and expanded many times in
later periods. Minor additions were made simply by
supplementing and reprinting the existing woodblocks,
but occasionally an entirely new edition was carved for
publication.[3] Because of Li Dongyang's immense prestige
as an official, literatus, and calligrapher, all later versions
reproduce his elegant running-script preface to the
original edition. Moreover, his daughter had married
Duke Kong Wenshao (1482–1546; acceded 1503), a liaison
that greatly enhanced the latter's clout.[4] The impetus for

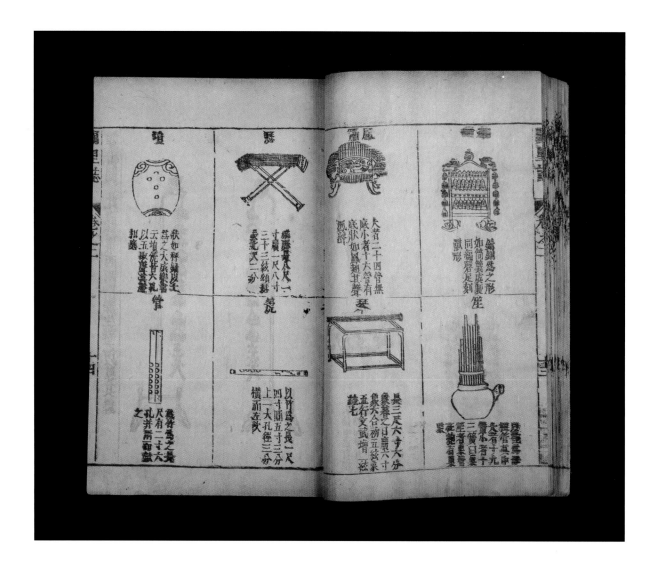

later editions came from Kong descendants, rather than civil service officials, and increasingly reflected lineage interests. A line drawing of the Qufu temple's sculptural icon of Confucius, virtually unique after the 1530 ritual reform, first appeared in the edition compiled in 1599 by sixty-third-generation descendant Kong Zhencong (active late 16th–early 17th c.).[5]

The exhibited edition of *Queli zhi* was compiled by Kong Yinzhi (1592–1647), who became the sixty-fifth-generation duke in 1621, during a period when ducal power was being challenged by other powerful families in the region.[6] He supplemented existing text and pictures from earlier versions and added new material at the end. However, the section on imperial bequests includes Qing entries dating through the second lunar month of 1724,

obviously added with supplementary woodblocks long after his lifetime. The blurry quality of the printing suggests that the blocks of this edition saw heavy use and became worn down. In this copy, the twenty-four *juan* are bound in ten volumes (*ce*) housed in a single wrapper.

The line drawing of the icon in the Hall of Great Accomplishment is labeled "Image of Confucius, the Great Accomplishment Ultimate Sage Culture-Propagating First Teacher" (*Dacheng zhisheng wenxuan xianshi Kongzi zhi xiang*), a title used only from 1645 to 1652. It portrays Confucius seated on a throne wearing imperial regalia, like the highest gods of Daoism and popular religion.[7] The circulation of this image eventually led ordinary people to treat Confucius as a god, one perhaps likely to help those seeking educational success.

JKM

1. For Li Dongyang's biography, see *Dictionary of Ming Biography*, pp. 877–81.

2. Chen Gao was responsible for overseeing students at government schools in Shandong and conducting the triennial *juren* examination. I have seen examples of his edition in Taipei at the National Library of China and National Palace Museum Library. The name Queli (Watchtower District) was first used in the Han period to refer to the temple of Confucius in Qufu; Ban Gu, *Hanshu*, *juan* 67, pp. 2925–26.

3. Chen Gao's 1505 edition contains entries dated up to 1520. A new edition in 15 *juan*, published in 1552 by 61st-generation descendant Kong Honggan, featured a bust-length version of the portrait of Confucius as minister of justice in Lu (see cat. no. 1); a reduced-facsimile of this gazetteer is reprinted in *Beijing tushuguan guji zhenben congkan*, vol. 23, pp. 393–897. For insightful analysis of the complex agendas behind the production of the gazetteers and the sometimes divergent interests of Kongs and regular civil service officials, see Agnew, "Culture and Power," esp. chap. 3. An administrative gazetteer representing Qufu in a dynasty-centered framework rather than from a Kong perspective appeared only with the publication of *Qufu xian zhi* in 1776, after the Kong duke lost the right to select the magistrate of Qufu.

4. See Agnew, "Culture and Power," pp. 106–8. As evidence, Agnew points out that after the Qufu county-government office was destroyed in 1511, Kong Wenshao got it rebuilt near the temple and mansion, and a new city wall also centered on the complex.

5. Kong Zhencong's 12-*juan* edition was not published until 1609. There are copies in the Naikaku Bunkō and Feng Ping Shan Library of the University of Hong Kong. Waseda University's faithful Japanese recut edition of 1669 is fully reproduced online at http://archive.wul.waseda.ac.jp/kosho/ru05/ru05_01635/.

6. Kong Yinzhi (*zi*, Duihuan) became duke in 1621. His name was later changed to Kong Yunzhi to avoid a taboo on the use of the Yongzheng emperor's personal name. Other examples of this edition are held in university libraries at Princeton, Chicago, Harvard, and Columbia; the National Library of China (Beijing and Taipei); and Naikaku Bunkō. Waseda University has reproduced its copy online at http://archive.wul.waseda.ac.jp/kosho/ru05/ru05_01581/. For a reduced-facsimile reprint, see *Siku quanshu cunmu congshu, Shi bu, Zhuanji lei*, series 2, vol. 76.

7. I discuss the consequences of these visual similarities in Murray, "'Idols' in the Temple," pp. 386–97.

4

Traces of the Sage (Pictorial Biography of Confucius)
明代　彩绘绢本圣迹图册

Ming dynasty (1368–1644)
Album of 36 paintings and 5 leaves of calligraphy; ink and color on silk
Each leaf: 33 × 57–62 cm (painting only); 40.8 × 66 cm (overall with mounting)
The Confucius Museum in Qufu, Shandong Province

COLOPHONS
Cheng Man 程漫 (18th c.), dated 1729
Wei Zhizhang 卫支彰 (18th c.), dated 1730

In addition to static portraits that depict him in a timeless, iconic mode, Confucius also appears in lively narrative pictures that show him interacting with disciples, feudal lords, and assorted other people whom he encountered over the course of his life. Although individual events were already being illustrated in the Eastern Han period, a linked set of pictures treating the entire life of Confucius was created only in the mid-fifteenth century. Generically known as "pictures of the Sage's traces" (*Shengji tu*), illustrated biographies evolved rapidly in the late Ming period as new versions with varying numbers of scenes were produced in a variety of media, including painting, woodblock-printing, and incised stone tablets.[1]

Often sponsored by government officials and other highly educated literati, pictorial biographies of Confucius enabled people to "see" him in action and contemplate his exemplary character. Late Qing and Republic-era woodblock and lithographic editions aimed to extend his appeal from the literate elite to a broader range of viewers. In a period when China's very survival as a nation was uncertain, sponsors of a 1934 edition asserted that pictures were an effective way of engaging people with Confucius, who was the essence of Chinese civilization.[2] Modern and contemporary treatments of his life have appeared more recently in such diverse new media as panels of carved colored stones, feature films, comic books, television series, and cartoons.[3]

The earliest pictorial biography of Confucius, completed in 1444, contained twenty-nine paintings based on events described in the *Shiji*.[4] Illustrated by an anonymous artist, the episodes were selected by a Ming censor, Zhang Kai (1398–1460), who also composed a poetic encomium (*zan*) containing eight four-character lines for each event. The series began with Confucius's mother praying for a son and ended with Han Gaozu's sacrifice at the Qufu temple in 195 BCE (see p.15, fig. 2). The biographical events that Zhang selected were ones that illuminated Confucius's moral character and personal qualities, his studies of rites and music, interactions with feudal lords and aristocrats, travels among the states, and mentoring of his disciples. To preserve the inspirational compendium and share it more widely, Zhang Kai had it reproduced as incised stone tablets, from which rubbings could be made and circulated.[5]

Although Zhang Kai's original versions appear not to survive, they inspired many later compilations that repeatedly changed the emphasis and tone of the illustrated narrative. A late fifteenth-century woodblock-printed expansion, reflected in the painted album displayed here, added nine scenes; these are readily identified because their texts do not include Zhang Kai's eight-line poems (compare scene 32 with the other seven exhibited here). The additions illustrated accounts of supernatural signs relating to Confucius's miraculous birth and his heavenly destiny to order the world, stories which do not figure in his *Shiji* biography but come from apocryphal texts (e.g., scene 32; see also p. 14, fig. 1).[6] The inclusion of pictures that portray a godlike Confucius probably reflects the influence of Buddhist and Daoist hagiography, which flourished in the later fifteenth century. Versions of Confucius's pictorial biography from the late sixteenth century onward added a four-character title to each scene and often included more episodes, as exemplified by the 112-picture version carved on stone tablets in the Hall of the Sage's Traces (Shengjidian) (see p. 21, fig. 6).[7]

Among painted versions of the *Pictures of the Sage's Traces* that survive today, this album is the earliest and finest. Probably dating to the sixteenth century, it includes the nine episodes that were added to the core group in the late fifteenth century. The unidentified artist seems to have based the paintings on a set of printed pictures without knowing the details of the events they illustrated, and occasionally a significant motif is inadvertently omitted from the composition. Nonetheless, he displays considerable flair in bringing the ancient anecdotes to life, using a palette of vivid colors. His figures are lively and expressive, even in crowds (e.g., scene 31), and the recurrent image of Confucius, with his grey robe and generally dour expression, is readily recognized from scene to scene. The artist seems to particularly relish the opportunity to portray men of low social status, whose uninhibited body language and déshabillé contrast with the disciplined decorum of Confucius and his disciples (e.g., scene 18).

The album bears no documentation other than two colophons by eighteenth-century Yangzhou literati, Cheng Man and Wei Zhizhang.[8] The absence of signatures or seals is not surprising, as the viewer was meant to be inspired more by the subject than by the artistry of its representation. In fact, Wei Zhizhang explicitly cautioned its new owner, a Yangzhou salt merchant named Wang Qinweng, not to put the pictures on a table together with miscellaneous objects for mere enjoyment. The work entered the collection of the Kong Mansion in Qufu some time after 1762, when Kong Jifen compiled a list of its paintings of Confucius.[9] The wide, rectangular format and variations in the widths of individual paintings suggest that the pictures may originally have been mounted as a handscroll.

Although the paintings in this set are not numbered or titled, their biographical sequence is usually clear because most of the accompanying texts mention a specific year for the event illustrated. For convenience, descriptive titles taken from equivalent scenes in other versions are often used in identifying them. The following leaves are included in the exhibition:

Scene 9: Confucius asks Laozi about the rites (cf. cat. no. 8).

With the aid of an aristocratic disciple, Nangong Jingshu, Confucius traveled to the Zhou capital (at Luoyang, Henan) to learn more about ritual and met Laozi, the archivist of the library.[10] The artist has imagined the encounter in terms of Ming material culture and social practices, adding servants who prepare tea, a large painted screen mounted in a heavy wooden frame, and books in contemporary binding. Nangong Jingshu appears larger than Confucius and sits in front, perhaps to indicate his higher social position. Four other disciples stand behind Confucius, the first appearance of what becomes a standard group of attendants in later scenes of this album. His ox-drawn cart also appears here for the first of many times, although Sima Qian's biography says that on this occasion, Confucius traveled in a carriage drawn by two horses supplied by the duke of Lu, who also sent the servant standing beside the parked vehicle.

Scene 10: Confucius hears the Shao music in the state of Qi.

When the duke of Lu was ousted in a coup, the thirty-five-year-old Confucius followed him to the neighboring state of Qi. There Confucius discussed music with the Qi grand master and heard the Shao music of sage-emperor Shun,

4-9

which he studied so ardently that he was oblivious to the taste of meat for three months. Duke Jing of Qi sought his advice on governance, and Confucius made his famous reply, "Rulers should be rulers, ministers should be ministers, fathers should be fathers, and sons should be sons."[11] The painting shows Confucius and the duke sitting side by side in front of a large painted screen in a palace courtyard. The duke gestures toward the standing master of music, who holds out an open book (anachronistic) as musicians prepare their instruments. These include a bell and V-shaped chime on separate stands (cf. cat. nos. 17–18), drum, zither (se), and mouth-organs (sheng). Confucius expresses his delight with a rare smile.

4-10

Scene 15: The execution of Shao Zhengmao.

In his fifties, Confucius finally gained substantive office in the state of Lu. After a successful year as a magistrate of the central district (*Zhongdu zai*), Duke Ding appointed him minister of works (*sikong*) and then minister of justice (*dasikou*), eventually assigning him the responsibilities of prime minister (cf. cat. no. 1). During this period, Confucius executed a high official, Shao Zhengmao, for creating chaos in the government. After three months, meat vendors stopped raising their prices, men and women stayed on different sides of the street, and no one took up things dropped accidentally on the road.[12] The illustration manages to refer to all of these details in an economically organized composition. Wearing an ornate multi-tiered headdress secured with a large horizontal pin, Confucius presides from a high-backed chair in front of a large screen and table loaded with bound books (all anachronistic). He gestures to two strongmen whose swords are raised to strike the kneeling Shao Zhengmao, held down by a third. Recalling paintings of the Kings of Hell, attendants stand nearby holding a rolled scroll and a book, and a third reads Shao's sentence from an open scroll. Behind this group, four women and two children stroll toward a cloth lying on the ground. On the other side of the road are assorted animals and six men, three of whom weigh meat on a scale while a fourth holds an account book. Two men with rolled umbrellas over their shoulders point toward a second piece of dropped clothing.

Scene 18: Confucius is rescued from the men of Kuang's siege.

After quitting the service of Duke Ding of Lu in disgust because the latter showed more interest in sensual indulgence than in maintaining correct ritual, Confucius went to other states seeking employment. When he passed through Kuang, the locals mistook him for a man from Lu whom they hated and detained him for five days. Although the disciples were afraid, Confucius proclaimed his belief in heaven's protection.[13] Nonetheless, the artist has given him a worried expression. Dressed once again in plain clothes, he sits in his parked cart, surrounded by menacing fighters wearing headwraps and stripped to the waist. Their droll expressions lend a comic touch, as they brandish weapons and fists in a choreographed display of martial arts. One disciple bows decorously toward them, accompanied by two others. Another disciple approaches Confucius with an open scroll. This is probably Yan Hui, who had arrived in the midst of the confrontation. The temporarily idled ox stands foursquare with his hindquarters facing the viewer.

Scene 31: Confucius and his disciples at the Apricot Terrace, studying rites and music.

After many years of traveling, Confucius was invited back to Lu at the age of sixty-eight. When he returned, however, no post was offered to him, so he devoted himself to editing and teaching the ancient texts. He wrote a preface to the *Documents* (*Shu*), transmitted the *Rites* (*Li*), arranged the *Odes* (*Shi*), corrected the *Music* (*Yue*), composed a preface and commentaries to the *Changes* (*Yi*), and completed a chronicle (*Chunqiu*). His students increased to three thousand, seventy-two of whom mastered the Six Arts.[14] The *Zhuangzi*, a text from the third century BCE, calls the place where they gathered "Apricot Terrace" (*Xingtan*) (see cat. nos. 6 and 7).[15] The illustration portrays a collegial gathering with the disciples talking or reading together, mostly in companionable groups of three. One stands with his back to the viewer to address a question to Confucius, who sits facing outward in front of a painted screen at a cloth-covered table, flanked by three pairs of disciples standing in respectful postures. The scene suggests the idyllic gathering of scholars at a Ming academy (see cat. no. 7).

Scene 32: Kneeling, Confucius receives a red rainbow from the Big Dipper.

This incident, attesting to heaven's approval of Confucius's editorial labors, comes not from Sima Qian's biography of Confucius but paraphrases an account in a thirteenth-century Kong genealogy, which in turn copies an apocryphal text.[16] After Confucius finished writing or editing the texts that would become the Classics, he fasted and purified himself at his study hall. Then facing the Northern Dipper, he performed an obeisance to announce their completion to heaven, and a red rainbow came down and transformed into yellow jade incised with an inscription. The painting shows him kneeling with his hands outstretched toward an altar, where an incense burner stands between vases of auspicious fungus (*lingzhi*). In the sky, a receding billow of clouds reveals a constellation recognizable as the Big Dipper, depicted as white circles connected by thin lines. A pale reddish arc sweeps across the cloud swirls and extends down almost to the altar. Pairs of disciples tend two side tables displaying three books each, and two more men stand behind Confucius, next to a screen with a blossoming plum and Taihu rock looming behind it. The setting evokes an elegant Ming garden with contemporary furnishings.

JKM

4-15

4-18

4-31

4-32

1. For much more detailed discussions than what is feasible here, see Murray, "Illustrations of the Life of Confucius" and "Varied Views of the Sage."

2. Comments of this sort are made by Jing Yaoyue (1881–after 1937) and Li Bingwei (?–after 1938) in their respective prefaces to *Kongzi shengji tu*, a lithographic edition published in 1934 by the Nation Society of Beiping (*Beiping minshe*), a "national essence" group concerned that modernization would cause China to abandon its cultural heritage.

3. Examples of each type of new medium include, respectively, a set of 36 large panels donated to the restored Nanjing Temple of Confucius (Fuzimiao) in 1998; the 1940 film *Kong Fuzi*, directed by Fei Mu (1906–1951) and recently screened by the Hong Kong Film Archive, as well as a movie starring Chow Yun-fat to be released in 2010; a comic book for ages 7 and up, simply called *Kongzi*, from the series *Hao ertong lizhi congshu*, vol. 14; a 2002 TV drama starring Wang Huichun; and a 104-episode series of 13-minute cartoons that started being broadcast in autumn 2009 on CCTV in China.

4. Sima Qian, *Shiji*, juan 47, pp. 1905–47. I discuss the origins of the pictorial biography at length in Murray, "Illustrations of the Life of Confucius."

5. The scholar and bibliophile Zheng Zhenduo (1898–1958), who owned several editions of the *Shengji tu*, speculated that Zhang Kai's original compendium was a woodblock-printed book; see *Zhongguo gudai banhua congkan*, preface. His observations on the filiation of later editions have been widely accepted and repeated in subsequent scholarship. However, in analyzing a large number of extant editions and consulting additional literary and historical evidence, I have come to very different conclusions. The wording of Zhang Kai's 1444 colophon suggests that his initial compilation was a painted handscroll, and his epitaph states that he had it reproduced as incised stones set into the walls of a courtyard at his house in Ningbo, which is independently confirmed by his great-great-grandson, Zhang Jiude (*jinshi*, 1601). For detailed discussion, see Murray, "Varied Views of the Sage" and "Illustrations of the Life of Confucius."

6. He Xun (*zi*, Tingrui; *jinshi*, 1457), prefect of Hengzhou, took the initiative to add episodes that he thought Zhang Kai had wrongly left out, and the new version was published as a woodblock-printed album. This in turn was copied and republished by others; see my most recent analysis of He's undertaking in Murray, *Mirror of Morality*, pp. 110–11.

7. Together with the tablets containing framing and commemorative texts, the entire set consists of 120 stones; I analyze its history and contents in detail in Murray, "The Temple of Confucius and Pictorial Biographies of the Sage."

8. The colophons by Cheng Man and Wei Zhizhang are reproduced in *Shengji zhi tu*, unpaginated. I have not found biographical information on either man nor on the album's owner, a Yangzhou salt merchant whom Wei refers to as Wang Qinweng (fl. ca. 1730).

9. Kong Jifen, *Queli wenxian kao*, juan 12, p. 11b (230).

10. Sima Qian, *Shiji*, juan 47, p. 1909. Excerpts transcribed on the paintings contain occasional variant characters or paraphrases compared with Sima Qian's version.

11. Ibid., pp. 1910–11.

12. Ibid., pp. 1915–17.

13. Ibid., p. 1919.

14. Ibid., pp. 1934–38.

15. *Zhuangzi jishi*, "Yufu pian" 31, p. 1023.

16. Kong Yuancuo, *Kongshi zuting guangji*, juan 9, pp. 10a–b. The story is recounted in the section on significant sites outside the Qufu temple, in the entry on Confucius's "study hall" (*xuetang*), located five *li* to the north. The account clearly draws on the earlier apocryphal text *Chunqiu yan Kong tu*; see discussion in Kaji Nobuyuki, *Kōshi gaden*, pp. 134–35. The text on the album leaf omits some of the details, notably the content of the inscription on the jade tablet. Another version of the story, which is even more elaborate and contains details that differ from Kong Yuancuo's account, appears in the Eastern Jin anthology *Soushen ji*, juan 8, p. 68; translated in *In Search of the Supernatural*, p. 108 (8.232).

5

Carved woodblock for printing *Traces of the Sage (Pictorial Biography of Confucius)*

明代晚期/清代早期　木刻圣迹图雕版

Late Ming or early Qing period, 17th century

Jujube wood (*zaomu*)

H. 30 cm, W. 53 cm, W. interior frame (*banxin*) 52.5 cm, D. 2.5 cm

The Confucius Museum in Qufu, Shandong Province

Many versions of the illustrated life of Confucius, often called *Shengji tu*, were produced in various parts of China from the late fifteenth to the twentieth century (see cat. no. 4). Several were published in Qufu itself, and numerous woodblocks used for printing them survive there today. In the late sixteenth century, concerns about unsystematic storage of woodblocks prompted the 1592 construction of the Hall of the Sage's Traces (Shengjidian), where a pictorial biography was incised on stone tablets to provide an orderly and permanent display. This late Ming representation of Confucius's life, installed in a building on the main axis of his home temple, quickly became authoritative and led to additional woodblock-printed editions based on it.

The exhibited block was used for printing the earliest edition to reproduce the stone tablets, a seventeenth-century edition whose compiler's name and circumstances of production are unknown.[1] The thorough blackening of the deeply carved but well-worn surfaces

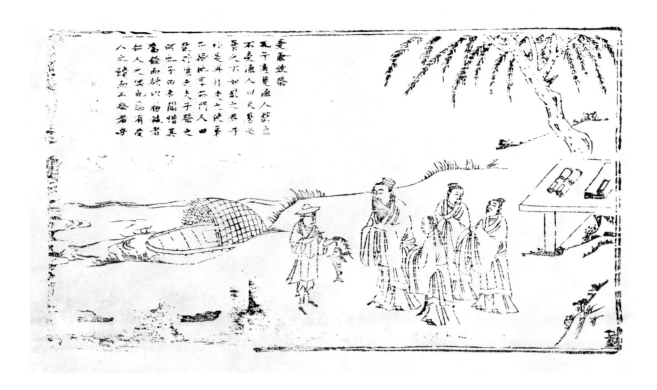

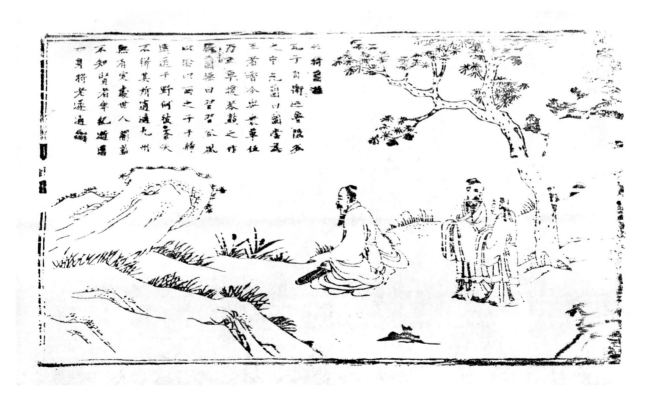

attests to repeated use of the block, as copies were printed from them to circulate the pictorial biography more widely. The number of illustrations in this edition was trimmed to 105 from the 112 belonging to the set in the Hall of the Sage's Traces. The same 105 compositions appear with only minor details changed in a recut edition published in 1874 by seventy-second-generation descendant Kong Xianlan (*juren*, 1862).[2]

Carved on both sides to conserve the valuable hardwood and use less storage space, the blocks for the seventeenth-century edition each contain two complete illustrations and their associated texts. The two on the exhibited block are among the large number of scenes that were added in the sixteenth century to earlier versions of the illustrated biography, and neither episode appears in the painted album also displayed here (cat. no. 4). Many episodes in the expanded set were instances in which Confucius discussed or demonstrated the moral conduct appropriate to a particular situation.

One side of this block, titled "Receiving a Fish and Offering Sacrifice" (*Shou yu zhi ji*), illustrates an anecdote in which Confucius explains the principle behind a point of behavior that at first seems illogical.[3] It tells of his encounter in the state of Chu with a fisherman who offered him a fish. At first he refused it. When the man said that it would otherwise spoil in the heat, Confucius changed his mind and accepted the fish. He told his disciples to prepare a sacrifice, but they objected that such a formal acknowledgement was inappropriate for food that had almost been thrown away. However, Confucius said that by giving away his surplus, the man showed that he was humane (*ren*), and one should always acknowledge the gift of a humane man by offering a sacrifice. The illustration simply shows a man holding out a fish toward Confucius, who is attended by three disciples. A moored boat, willow tree, and table with two scrolls and an anachronistically bound book complete the composition.

The other side of the block is carved with a scene titled "Composing [the song] 'Oh! The Orchid'" (*Zuo Yi lan cao*). When Confucius was returning to Lu from the state of Wei, he passed through a hidden valley where orchids were growing. Commenting that the orchid should be the fragrance of kings but nowadays had become associated with the masses of ordinary plants, he stopped his carriage and picked up his zither (*qin*). Strumming it, he composed a song lamenting that the world was in disorder and worthies [such as himself] went unrecognized.[4] Ending on the gloomy note that he was getting old and would soon die, he went back to Wei.

In the picture, Confucius sits on ground playing the zither and gazing toward orchid plants growing near a large rock. Behind him, under a luxuriant pine, two disciples stand in attendance and exchange glances.

Among the other sets of woodblocks in Qufu is one for an edition dateable to the Qianlong period (mid-eighteenth century); it contains finely carved pictures but no texts, which evidently were added on the printed copy in handwritten calligraphy. In 1934, the Beijing-based "Nation Society" (Beiping minshe) published a lithographic reproduction of that edition under the title *Kongzi shengji tu*, which has been reissued repeatedly in recent years.[5] According to the order of scenes in that work, the two illustrations on the block exhibited here are numbers 75 and 83, respectively.

JKM

1. Many copies of this edition have survived. It includes Zhang Yingdeng's 1592 dedicatory inscription for the Shengjidian tablets (see above, p. 21), leading some libraries to erroneously attribute that date to the printed version. According to a label accompanying a set of recent printings from the blocks, which was exhibited in the Kuiwen'ge in 1994, just 101 are extant today. For further discussion, see Murray, "Illustrations of the Life of Confucius," pp. 114–15 and Appendix C2–C5.

2. There are also many copies of this edition, titled *Xinkan Shengji tu ji*; see Murray, "Illustrations of the Life of Confucius," p. 115 and Appendix C10. I discuss its context and purpose in Murray, "Varied Views of the Sage," pp. 247–48. English translations of the texts appear in *An Illustrated Life of Confucius*.

3. The anecdote is from *Kongzi jiayu, juan* 2, p. 12, "Zhisi di ba" [Giving rein to thoughts, part 8]; see translation in Kramers, *K'ung Tzŭ Chia Yü*, pp. 231–32.

4. The opening couplet of the song is also the start of the poem "Gu feng," the lament of a rejected wife, in the *Classic of Poetry* (*Shijing*), one of the Confucian Classics; translated in Legge, *The She King*, pp. 55–58.

5. The 1934 Beiping minshe version of the pictorial biography omitted a controversial episode in which Confucius paid a courtesy call on Nanzi, the wife of Duke Ling of Wei; it also included photographs of Qufu and related material. Facsimile reprints include those published in Taipei, 1984, and (without original prefaces) Shijiazhuang, 1996. Reprints of just the pictorial biography (usually with one or more scenes missing) include editions published under the same title, *Kongzi shengji tu*, in Ji'nan (1988), Tianjin (1996), and Beijing (2005); a version with the same pictures but titled *Kongzi xingjiao tu* was published in Taipei, 1974. There are undoubtedly others.

6

Anonymous

***Confucius, Yan Hui, and Zeng Can* (with robes formed from characters of the *Analects*)**

明代　孔子、颜回、曾参三圣像　立轴

Ming dynasty (1368–1644)

Hanging scroll; ink on silk

143 × 75.5 cm (painting); 274 × 107 cm (overall with mounting)

The Confucius Museum in Qufu, Shandong Province

Spurious signature and partly effaced date at lower left:
　"Reverently sketched by Zhao Mengfu of Wuxing in the middle month of spring, third year of Dade [1299]" (*Dade san nian zhongchun Wuxing Zhao Mengfu jin xie* 大德三年仲春吴兴赵孟頫谨写)

Under the vine-draped bough of a pine tree, Confucius sits between two disciples who stand in attendance, their hands raised in a gesture of respect. Most unusually, the three men's robes are formed from tiny Chinese characters in regular script, each about four millimeters tall, which transcribe the first half of the *Analects* (*Lunyu*). Carefully written within tiny gridlines, the text begins on Confucius's left elbow (viewer's right) with the well-known sentence, "The Master said, 'To study and at times to practice what one has learned, is it not a pleasure?'" (*Zi yue, xue er shi xi zhi, bu yi yue hu*).

Although unlabeled, the flanking figures are customarily identified as two of Confucius's closest followers who are frequently mentioned in the *Analects*. To his right (viewer's left) is his favorite disciple, Yan Hui, and to his left (viewer's right) is Zengzi, who was believed to have played a particularly important role in transmitting Confucius's teachings.[1] By the Ming dynasty, Yan Hui was called the Returning Sage (Fusheng) and Zengzi the Ancestral Sage (Zongsheng), and both received regular sacrifices as two of the Four Correlates (*sipei*) of Confucius.

The nearly symmetrical arrangement of the three figures probably owes some of its inspiration to the visual conventions of the ubiquitous icons depicting the Buddha flanked by smaller *bodhisattvas*. Buddhist images may also have provided a precedent for composing a pictorial icon from the characters of a holy text, literally embodying its words.[2] The *Analects* is a collection of many separate passages recording Confucius's discussions with his disciples, and the text conveys a vivid sense of his personality, values, and teachings. Memorized by young scholars in traditional China, it was

one of the Four Books compiled by Zhu Xi as an introduction to Confucian learning (see cat. no. 11).

Confucius is shown wearing an angular hat secured by a large pin, the formal headgear associated with his brief service as minister of justice in Lu, which was the highest rank he attained in life (see cat. no. 1). His figure is notably larger than those of the two disciples, indicating not only his importance but also his

Detail

nearly identical to this painting, differing only in the appearance of the *Analects* characters on just the fold-lines and not the broad surfaces of the robes.[6] Kong Jifen's itemization of the painted portraits of Confucius that were in the Kong family collection by 1762 mentions only the unsigned work, suggesting that the "Zhao Mengfu" version was acquired afterward.

The use of the *Analects* in the visual arts is a continuing tradition. The Shandong artist Shi Ke (b. 1924) has gained fame for a series of 100 seals that he designed and carved with phrases selected from the *Analects*.[7] More recently, Qufu opened a city park, the Steles of the Analects Park (Lunyu bei yuan), that features stone tablets presenting well-known sayings from the venerable classic, set among pavilions and ponds.

JKM

exceptional height. According to Sima Qian, Confucius was over nine feet tall, and his descendants claimed that he had forty-nine unusual physical features (surpassing Sakyamuni Buddha's thirty-two).[3]

The stone platform on which Confucius rests his feet alludes to his teaching at the Apricot Terrace.[4] Brushed in broad strokes of pale inkwash, its rough surface echoes the impressionistic trunk of the bending pine. Such a deliberate contrast between the spontaneous brushwork of the abbreviated setting and the meticulously controlled, fine-lined representation of the figures is reminiscent of Yuan paintings in the Chan idiom.[5]

In the lower left corner of the painting are a spurious signature and seal of the renowned Yuan calligrapher and painter Zhao Mengfu (1254–1322) and a partially effaced date corresponding to the third lunar month of 1299. The Kong Mansion also owns an unsigned version that is

1. Zhu Xi described the process of the text's transmission in his preface to the *Constant Mean* (*Zhongyong*); see Gardner, introduction to *The Four Books*, and Tillmann, "Zhu Xi's Prayers to the Spirit of Confucius," p. 503.

2. A Ming example is a hanging scroll of Guanyin in the National Palace Museum, Taipei, which depicts the *bodhisattva* with the text of the "Universal Gate" (*Pumen pin*) chapter of the *Lotus Sutra*; see Clunas, *Empire of Great Brightness,* p. 96 and p. 97, fig. 74.

3. Sima Qian, *Shiji, juan* 47, p. 1905; Kong Chuan, *Dongjia zaji, juan xia*, p. 3b (108).

4. When 45th-generation descendant Kong Daofu rebuilt the Qufu Temple of Confucius in 1022, he installed a stone platform and planted apricot trees around the site where Confucius was thought to have lectured. A pavilion was added in the late twelfth century, during the Jin dynasty. Ground plans of the Qufu temple under the Song and Jin dynasties show the change; see Kong Yuancuo, *Kongshi zuting guangji, tu ben*, plates 8 and 10.

5. See Helmut Brinker, "Ch'an Portraits in a Landscape," *Archives of Asian Art* 27 (1973–74): 8–29.

6. It is apparently this somewhat simpler painting, not the "Zhao Mengfu" version, that Kong Jifen recorded in his 1782 inventory, under the title *Practicing the Teaching* (*Xingjiao xiang*); see Kong Jifen, *Queli wenxian kao, juan* 12, p. 11b (230). For reproductions, see *Da zai Kongzi*, pp. 97–98; *Kongzi xiang, Yanshenggong ji furen xiaoxiang*, plate 5; Luo Chenglie, *Huaxiang zhong de Kongzi*, plate 60; *Qufu Kongmiao, Konglin, Kongfu*, p. 193; *Temple and Cemetery of Confucius and the Kong Family Mansion in Qufu*, p. 126; or *Tianxia diyi jia*, p. 50, plates 84–85.

7. Reproduced in Shi Ke, *Kongzi shiji tu, Lunyu zhenyan yin*, pp. 43–94, and scattered through *Da zai Kongzi*.

7

Anonymous

Confucius Lecturing to His Disciples

明代　孔子讲学图　立轴

Ming dynasty (1368–1644)

Hanging scroll; ink and color on silk

167.5 × 85 cm (painting only); 301 × 118 cm
(overall with mounting)

The Confucius Museum in Qufu, Shandong
Province

Spurious signature, "Li Tang" 李唐 (ca. 1050–
after 1130), at lower left.

Seal (upper left):

Shaoxing 绍兴 (Song Gaozong reign
period, 1130–1162; intaglio [spurious])

Seals (lower left):

Da guan 大观 (Song Huizong reign period,
1107–1110; relief [spurious])

[Undeciphered] (unidentifed; relief)

Xiang Zijing jia zhen cang 项子京家珍藏
(Xiang Yuanbian 项元汴, 1525–1590;
relief [spurious])

Seal (middle right):

Kuaiji taishou zhang 会稽太守章 (seal of
the prefect of Kuaiji, Zhejiang [unidentified],
18th c.; intaglio)[1]

Seals (lower right):

Tang Bohu 唐伯虎 (Tang Yin 唐寅, 1470–1524;
relief [spurious])

Zhang Yan si yin 张燕私印 (Zhang Yan
张燕 [unidentified], Qing dynasty; intaglio)

This large and detailed composition portrays Confucius interacting with his disciples in an outdoor setting. Depicting him with a full beard that suggests late middle age, the scene refers to the period after he returned from his travels among the states of north China. For fourteen years, Confucius had searched for an ideal ruler who would employ him and heed his advice to govern with benevolence and proper ritual. After giving up this quest, Confucius returned to Lu and devoted himself to editing texts and teaching an ever-growing cohort of followers. During the Song dynasty, the spot where Confucius allegedly congregated with his disciples was commemorated with a stone platform, known as the Apricot Terrace (Xingtan), to which a pavilion was later added in the Jin dynasty.[2]

In a clearing framed by protruding rocks and an overhanging pine, Confucius sits on a tiger skin spread over a large, flat-topped stone. Wearing an elaborate official headdress, referring to his brief service as minister of justice in Lu (see cat. no. 1), he holds a curved *ruyi* scepter and rests against an ornate low table. His disproportionately large figure forms the apex of a triangle with the four disciples in the upper part of the painting. As three stand attentively to one side, one holding a small incense burner, the fourth bows low before Confucius to ask a question. Confucius responds with a benign gaze and extends his open hand in a gesture of encouragement.

Below, on a steep slope that curves around a waterfall, sixteen other men in voluminous robes are coming to join the gathering. Loosely clustered into three groups, they turn conversationally toward one another, and two seem to look out at the viewer. One man in each group is carrying a rolled-up scroll, and the lead figure holds a zither over his shoulder, protecting it with his sleeve. Some wear formal headgear and others cloth caps, perhaps to distinguish disciples who became officials from those who never served. The unknown artist took care to individualize the figures, giving them distinct facial expressions and gestures.

A notation along the lower left edge identifies the painter as Li Tang, a master of figures and landscape who served at court at the end of the Northern Song and beginning of the Southern Song periods. However, the arrangement of rather fanciful landscape elements into a visually dynamic pattern suggests a Ming artist of the later Zhe school. Rather than portraying an organic and naturalistic setting, the scene is a composite of conventional motifs, including a distant waterfall in upper right, as well as auspicious pine, cypress, bamboo, and blossoming apricot in the middle ground. Techniques

such as the streaky texture strokes on the rocks and mountain peaks recall Zhe-school interpretations of later Southern Song academic traditions of landscape.

The collegial gathering in an auspicious outdoor setting also evokes the ideals of the Ming private academy (*shuyuan*) movement, which experienced a major resurgence in the sixteenth century. To some extent a reaction against the intellectual sterility of government schools, particularly among followers of Wang Yangming (1472–1529), academies brought scholars and officials together for lectures and discussion. Often sited in scenic or historic locales, away from the pressing demands of public affairs, such retreats fostered self-cultivation and fraternal relationships.

Although its early history is unknown, the painting was in the collection of the Duke for Perpetuating the Sage by 1762, when it appeared in Kong Jifen's inventory.[3] Itemizing the handful of portraits of Confucius in the Kong Mansion's possession, he listed it as *Portrait [of Confucius] Lecturing on Ritual at the Apricot Terrace* and described it in sufficient detail to identify it with the present painting.

JKM

1. This seal was carved by Lin Gao (b. 1657; alternate name Hetian), a Fujian master active in Yangzhou, who carved seals for Wang Hui, Wu Li, Yun Shouping, Wang Hongxu, et al.; see ThinkQuest 2001 (Team CO124441) http://library.thinkquest.org/C0124441/b5index.php?nlv1=6&lv2=D&nlv3=5&nowleft=lv3 [accessed 6/30/09].
2. For details, see cat. no. 6, note 4.
3. Kong Jifen, *Queli wenxian kao, juan* 12, p. 11b (230).

8
Pictorial stone depicting Confucius Meets Laozi and Xiang Tuo and other scenes
东汉　孔子见老子及項橐画像石
Eastern Han dynasty (25–220)
Limestone
H. 110.5 cm, W. 48 cm, D. 19 cm
Shandong Provincial Museum

Confucius and his disciples frequently appear in the Han funerary art of southwestern Shandong, the region around his ancient home in Lu. The depiction of these exemplary figures on pictorial stones inside a tomb or offering shrine suggests that the values associated with them were endorsed by the deceased and his family. The upper register of this slab conflates two stories about Confucius, while the lower one depicts mounted warriors.

The scene at upper right (see rubbing, fig. 8-1) represents Confucius's encounters with the elderly ritual expert Laozi and the boy-genius Xiang Tuo. Identified by oblong cartouches, the two men bow deeply to one another as Confucius reaches toward the much shorter Xiang Tuo. The child appears to be offering a bird to Confucius with one hand and pushing a toy with the other. The figures further to the left include the brash disciple Zilu, typically portrayed with his sleeves flapping, and the diminutive Yanzi, wise minister of the neighboring state of Qi, who is labeled in the leftmost cartouche.

According to Sima Qian, Confucius went to the Zhou capital to learn about ancient rituals from Laozi, the aged Keeper of the Archives.[1] When they parted, Laozi warned Confucius that he would bring difficulties on himself if he criticized others too forthrightly.[2] Other dialogues between the two men are recorded in the *Zhuangzi*, which compares Confucius's political engagement unfavorably with Laozi's endorsement of non-action.

In contrast to his detailed account of Confucius's interactions with Laozi, Sima Qian barely mentions the

8-1

encounter with Xiang Tuo, saying only that the seven-year-old was Confucius's teacher.[3] Other texts present the anecdote as evidence that Confucius was not too proud to learn from anyone who had something to teach him, regardless of age or status.[4] The conflation of the two encounters appears on numerous relief-carved stones from the mid to late second century, its popularity perhaps reflecting an increased emphasis on scholarly virtue as a qualification for public office.[5]

In this example, the figures appear in profile as stately silhouettes in uniform low relief against an empty background where the stone is slightly cut away and striated, a contrast even more visible in the rubbing. Further distinctions are made between the decorous postures of the gentlemen in the upper band and the galloping horsemen with composite bows in the lower register, six of whom twist around to launch their arrows in a "Parthian shot." Linear details are economically incised on the flat surfaces to suggest facial features and clothing patterns. The style is typical of second-century pictorial art in the Jiaxiang area, not far from Qufu, of which the stones from the Wu Family Cemetery are the best known examples.[6]

JKM

1. Sima Qian, *Shiji, juan* 47, p. 1909; *juan* 63, p. 2140.
2. Martin Powers interprets this advice as referring to the upright official's right and responsibility to speak out against wrongs, despite danger to himself; *Art and Political Expression in Early China*, pp. 203–5. Michael Nylan points out the entertaining as well as didactic qualities of the pictorial stone's combination of anecdotal references; see her entry in Cary Liu et al., *Recarving China's Past*, cat. no. 10.
3. Sima Qian, *Shiji, juan* 71, p. 2319.
4. For detailed discussions, see Soymié, "L'entrevue de Confucius et de Hiang T'o"; Spiro, *Contemplating the Ancients*, pp. 23–31; and Kinney, *Representations of Childhood and Youth in Early China*, pp. 39–41.
5. For other examples from Shandong, see Li Jinshan, *Lunan Han huaxiang shi yanjiu*, pp. 363–66; also *Zhongguo huaxiang shi quanji*, vol. 1, plate 228, and vol. 2, plates 97, 99, 101, 115, 131, and 139.
6. See Cary Liu et al., *Recarving China's Past*.

9
Anonymous
Confucius Observes the Tilting Vessels
明代　孔子观敧器图　立轴

Ming dynasty (1368–1644)
Hanging scroll; ink and color on silk
99.5 × 59 cm (painting only)
269 × 89.5 cm (overall with mounting)
The Confucius Museum in Qufu, Shandong Province

Text, transcription of *Kongzi jiayu, juan* 2, section 9,
"Three Ways of Reciprocity" (*Sanshu di jiu* 三恕第九):

孔子观于鲁桓公之庙，有敧器焉．问于守庙者曰：
"此谓何器？"对曰："此盖为宥坐之器．"孔子曰：
"吾闻宥坐之器，虚则敧，中则正，满则覆，明君以
为至诚，故常置之于坐侧．"顾谓弟子曰："试注水
焉．"乃注之，水中则正，满则覆．夫子喟然叹曰：
"呜呼！夫物有满而不覆者哉？"子路进曰："敢问
持满有道乎？"子曰："聪明睿智，守之以愚；功被
天下，守之以让；勇力振世，守之以怯；富有四海，
守之以谦．此所谓损之又损之之道也．"

Seals: [Undeciphered] (unidentified; intaglio)

[Undeciphered] (unidentified; intaglio)

[Undeciphered] (unidentified; intaglio)

Xiang Molin fu miji zhiyin 项墨林父秘笈之印 (Xiang Yuanbian 项元汴，1525–1590; relief)

This painting illustrates an anecdote, versions of which appear in a number of early texts, in which Confucius explains the virtue of moderation. The passage that is transcribed above the scene comes from the *Sayings of the Confucians* (*Kongzi jiayu*) and may be paraphrased as follows: When Confucius was in the ancestral temple of Duke Huan of Lu (r. 711–694 BCE), he observed a tilting container and asked the temple guardian what it was. The custodian responded that it must be a cautionary vessel for beside the seat (*youzuo zhi qi*). Confucius had heard that enlightened rulers kept such containers beside their seats as an admonition, because when the vessel was empty, it tilted; when medium full, it was upright; and when filled up, it overturned. He then told his disciples to try pouring water into the vessel, and it responded as he had said. Thereupon Confucius sighed and asked whether there was anything that would not overturn when full (perhaps alluding to Duke Huan's lack

此天路日富大物之水孔
所下進明有有之為子
謂守日睿道道注觀
損之敬智子子之於
之以問守謂謂中桓
又讓持之夫守則公
損勇滿以子廟正之
之力而愚胡者
道振不功為此水滿
也世霸破明謂則則
守破君溢溢
之以以傾則則
法為為正則敢中
富至誠滿問
有誠明則此
四則君覆為
海襄子虛何
之明無則器
守則傾仰也
以危孔子對
謙正子顏曰

of restraint).[1] The disciple Zilu inquired whether there was a way to maintain fullness (without overturning; i.e., going to excess), leading Confucius to expound a series of positive qualities that are kept in check by a dash of their opposites: intelligence by stupidity, bravery by fear; wealth by modesty, etc. He ends by proclaiming, "This is called the way of decreasing and again decreasing."[2]

The artist has ignored the Daoist philosophizing at the end of this anecdote and treated the visual element of the homily with pedagogical clarity, as if illustrating a physics lesson on the effects of different amounts of water. Nothing is seen of the temple interior except a large red-lacquer stand, topped by a crystal ball. From the ornamental bar hang three separate containers resembling bronze bells decorated with bands of geometric ornament and attached to metal chains at different angles. Water cascades from the overturned vessel at left into an intricately carved marble trough. The custodian stands beside it, watching intently, and holds an ordinary wooden bucket that presumably supplied water for the demonstration (a minor contradiction with the text).

In the foreground, Confucius and Zilu bend toward one another in dialogue, and two other disciples stand in respectful attendance. None of the men looks toward the vessels. The simple juxtaposition of the two scenes suggests that the artist may have based his composition on earlier versions that illustrated the three positions of the containers separately from the conversations in the temple.[3] Depictions of the story can be traced back to the Southern Song period, if not earlier, and a variety of extant or recorded examples from later periods attest to its continued popularity.[4]

Although the painting now bears no attribution, the published version of Kong Jifen's 1762 inventory lists it as by a Ming artist named Guo Yi, probably meaning Guo Xu 郭诩 (1456–after 1526).[5] The unsigned text above the picture is written in a fluent style of regular script influenced by Southern Song imperial calligraphy. Each character occupies a square of a finely ruled grid that is centered over the painting.

JKM

1. Duke Huan of Lu murdered his elder brother and met his own violent death in the neighboring state of Qi. His sons were the progenitors of the three ministerial clans (Ji, Meng, and Shu) who usurped the Lu duke's powers, and Confucius opposed their breaches of proper ritual.
2. *Kongzi jiayu, juan* 2, p. 19, "Sanshu di jiu" [Three ways of reciprocity, part 9]; see translation in Kramers, *K'ung Tzŭ Chia Yü*, pp. 241 and 340–42. Other well-known versions of the story are in the *Xunzi, Huainanzi,* and *Hanshi waizhuan.*
3. For example, an early Ming reprint of a 13th-century illustrated edition of the *Xunzi,* published in Fujian under

the title *Zuantu huzhu Xunzi,* includes an illustration of three large and ornate containers on separate low tables; it is reproduced and discussed by Knoblock, "The History of the *Xunzi* Text." See also the facsimile reprint of *Zuantu huzhu Xunzi* in *Zhongguo zixue mingzhu jicheng,* vol. 24. An early 16th-century woodblock-printed *Shengji tu* in the Harvard Art Museum devotes two separate pages to the story: the first shows Confucius talking to the temple guardian, attended by one disciple [Zilu?] and four others next to his horse and carriage, while two servants bring a water-pail and shallow dish; the second is a closeup diagram of vessels in three positions, without any setting. See Murray, "Illustrations of the Life of Confucius," p. 89 and fig. 14. Versions of the *Shengji tu* from the late sixteenth century onward conflate the dialogue and the demonstration into one scene that includes a view of the temple building and sometimes just one vessel.
4. Besides the various *Shengji tu* noted above, there was an anonymous Yuan hanging scroll recorded by Yuan literatus Chen Lü in *Anyatang ji, juan* 13, pp. 4b–5a (164–65). The Korean *Veritable Records* for the year 1433 mentions a mural in the imperial palace; see An Hwi-jun, *Chosŏn wangjo sillok ŭi sŏhwa saryo,* p. 36.
5. Kong Jifen, *Queli wenxian kao, juan* 12, p. 11b (230). The two characters look alike in cursive and semi-cursive script, and a mistake could have occurred when his notes were transcribed during the woodblock-printing process. Guo Xu (*zi,* Renhong; *hao,* Qingkuang), a native of Taihe, Jiangxi, enjoyed a national reputation and was said to rank with Du Jin, Wu Wei, and Shen Zhou; see Yu Jianhua, *Zhongguo meishujia renming cidian,* p. 956. The majority of Gu's extant figural works display a rough and spontaneous mode unlike the present painting; however, like Du Jin and Wu Wei, he also had a fine style.

10

Music, Dance, and 100 Entertainments; Queen Mother of the West; and Lecturing on the Classics
东汉乐舞百戏画像石拓片
Modern rubbing of Eastern Han dynasty (25–220) stone
Ink on paper
82.7 x 83 cm
Shandong Provincial Museum

Pictorial stone carvings are commonly found on the outer coffin chamber of stone tombs belonging to the Eastern Han aristocracy and bureaucratic elite, as well as in their above-ground offering shrines. They are mainly found distributed in four regions: the southern part of the old Lu state (consisting of present-day southern Shandong, northern Jiangsu, and northeastern Anhui), Henan, northern Shaanxi, and Sichuan. Those found in southern Shandong are particularly rich and diverse in their carving

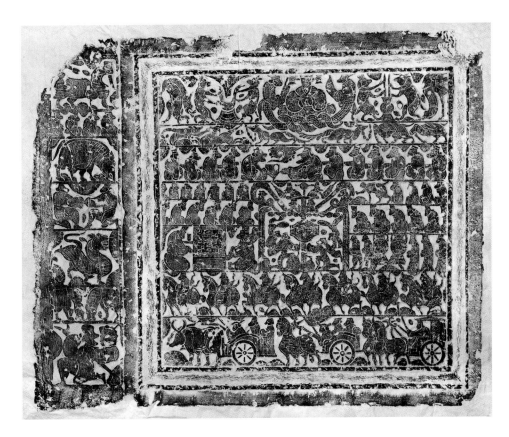

techniques, which include sculptural relief, openwork, engraved line, striated-ground flat relief, and so on. The contents of the pictorial stone carvings found in southern Shandong are also extremely rich, including subjects from the mythology of the celestial kingdom to human activities, animals and plants, and floral motifs and geometric patterns of all kinds. The carvings can be said to constitute an encyclopedia of Eastern Han imagery.

The surface of this pictorial stone is divided into eight registers. At the top is "Ascending to Immortality." In Chinese legends, the Queen Mother of the West is the paramount female deity. The Western Zhou dynasty sovereign, King Mu, was said to have met the Queen Mother when paying homage to her by the celestial Yaochi Lake, located in present-day Tianshan Mountains in the western region of Xinjiang. The two figures with entwined serpentine tails are Fuxi and Nuwa, the progenitors of the human race in Chinese mythology. They were said to have been brother and sister, but after the Great Flood there were no human survivors on earth except the two of them. In compliance with the will of the gods, they became husband and wife and gave birth to children who were the ancestors of mankind. The rabbit pounding medicinal herbs was an attendant to the Queen Mother of the West. According to mythology, the

rabbit later became Chang E's companion when she ascended to live in her lonely palace on the moon; he is responsible for the production of the elixir of immortality.

The second register features auspicious beasts, including the nine-tailed fox, that are all members of the Queen Mother's entourage. Their presence is a sign of the celestial realm of the Western Heavens. The third register is a depiction of lecturing on the Classics. At the center, two Confucian scholars holding books in the form of bamboo strips are represented with their mouths open as if discoursing the Classics, an extremely vivid illustration of a teaching scenario.

The fourth through sixth registers are filled with pictures of dance and acrobatics. Erected at the center is a drum tower, around which dancers and musicians perform and chess players compete in front of an audience. Registers seven and eight feature a cavalcade of chariots and mounted riders. The images from registers three through eight reflect various aspects in the extravagant lifestyle of the nobility at the time. Overall, the eight registers present a grand and imposing scene, especially with the picture of ascending to immortality, expressing the ideal of a perfect dream world in the afterlife of the master.

LWS

11

*The Four Books with Collected
Annotations (Sishu jizhu)*
明代 《四书集注》(吉简王朱見浚吉府刻本)

Ming dynasty, 1480
Woodblock-printed book (2 volumes displayed)
Each volume: H. 29.9 cm, W. 18.7 cm, D. 1 cm
Shandong Provincial Museum

Publisher's cartouche and date: "Republished in Jifu in
[1480]" (*Chenghua gengzi, Jifu chongkan*
成化庚子吉府重刊).

Seals: *Jifu tushu* 吉府图书 (Zhu Jianjun 朱見浚, the Ming
Prince of Ji, 1456–1527; relief)

Wanxiangtang zhencang 晚香堂珍藏
(unidentified; intaglio)

Confucius himself claimed that he was merely a teacher
and transmitter of ancient rituals and history, not a creator
or philosopher. Nonetheless, he was traditionally regarded
as the author, compiler, or editor of the "Confucian
Classics," which vary in number from five to fourteen,
depending on the period and criteria used in counting.[1]

During the eleventh and twelfth centuries, scholars
associated with the School of the Way (*Daoxue*), often
called Neo-Confucians, singled out four texts as the
essential core of the Confucian canon: the *Great Learning*

(*Daxue*), the *Analects* (*Lunyu*; see cat. no. 6), the *Mencius*
(*Mengzi*), and the *Constant Mean* (*Zhongyong*).[2] These
works contained the most succinct and direct teachings
of the ancient sages. Their most influential exponent,
Zhu Xi (1130–1200), selected earlier scholars' annotations
and wrote commentaries for the four texts, which he
published as a set in 1190. Arranged in a deliberate
sequence, with each line of the main text accompanied
by notes to prompt the reader's engagement and
reflection, Zhu Xi's Four Books constitute a program of
moral self-cultivation. After mastering it, the student
could go on to the other classics. Potentially accessible
to all, the Four Books embody foundational values of
Chinese civilization.

Zhu Xi's arrangement of the Four Books spread
quickly and widely in Southern Song government schools
and private academies through the efforts of his numerous
disciples, and it soon became authoritative.[3] In 1313, the
Yuan emperor officially designated it as the official
curriculum of the civil service examinations. The texts and
commentaries were memorized by generation after
generation of young men who aspired to government
careers, until the examination system was abolished in the
early twentieth century. From Zhu Xi's lifetime onward,
many versions of the Four Books were published. The
imperial court, government schools, private academies,
and commercial publishers all produced editions and at
varying levels of quality and cost.[4]

The example exhibited here was published by Zhu
Jianjun (1456–1527), the first Ming Prince of Ji, in his
domain (called Jifu) at Changsha, Hunan.[5] The sharp
detail, large typeface, and generous margins of the
printing reflect the sumptuous standards set by
publications produced in the early Ming palace.[6] Because
the prince's colophon explicitly refers to his edition as a
1480 recarving, the blocks were probably based on a
printed example from the central court.

Other projects sponsored by Zhu Jianjun suggest that he
had more than average interest in Confucian ideals and
learning. In 1497, he published a set of annotated illustrations
of the life of Confucius, also copied from a recently printed
edition.[7] Titled *Kongzi shengji zhi tu*, the deluxe publication
eventually found its way to Japan, where it inspired several
new versions in the Edo period (1603–1867). The prince also
had an edition of the *Book of Documents* (*Shangshu*) cut at
Changsha's celebrated Marchmount Academy (Yuelu
shuyuan), an institution that Zhu Xi himself had helped to
invigorate in the late twelfth century.[8]

JKM

1. For an overview, see M. H. Kim and Michael Loewe, "Confucian Classics," in *RoutledgeCurzon Encyclopedia of Confucianism*, vol. 1, pp. 86–90, or the introduction to Gardner, *The Four Books*.

2. The *Great Learning* and the *Constant Mean* were originally chapters in the larger *Book of Rites* (*Liji*); for translations and discussion, see Plaks, *Ta Hsüeh and Chung Yung*. Gardner provides an excellent introduction to all four in *The Four Books*.

3. On Zhu Xi's role in the academy movement, see Walton, *Academies and Society in Southern Sung China*, esp. chap. 2.

4. Although Southern Song editions have survived above ground, the earliest known excavated example was commercially published in 1362 in Hangzhou and found in the tomb of the Ming prince Zhu Tan (1370–1390) near Qufu; for the excavation report, see Shandong sheng bowuguan, "Fajue Ming Zhu Tan mu jishi." The work has recently been reproduced in facsimile by the Beijing Library. See Zhu Xi, *Sishu zhangju jizhu*; for sample pages of the original, see *Confucius: À l'aube de l'humanisme chinois*, p. 79.

5. The seventh son of Yingzong (r. 1435–49 and 1457–64), Zhu Jianjun gained his title in 1457 and moved to his domain in 1477; his extravagant construction projects there were criticized in the early 1490s. For biographical information, see *Mingshi*, *juan* 119, p. 3637; ibid., *juan* 194, p. 5137; and *Gujin tushu jicheng*, *ce* 346, *juan* 72, p. 24a.

6. See Jang, "The Eunuch Agency Directorate of Ceremonial and the Ming Imperial Publishing Enterprise," esp. pp. 125–29. By contrast, the characters on the pages of the late Yuan commercial edition buried with Zhu Tan (see note 4) are cramped and crowded together.

7. See cat. no. 4, note 6. Examples of the Jifu reprint exist in the National Library of China, Beijing (Rare Book 14385) and Harvard Art Museum (1985.842); pages from the latter are reproduced in Murray, "Illustrations of the Life of Confucius," figs. 5–7 and 9–14. Like the *Four Books* here, this work also displays a *Jifu tushu* seal and *Jifu chongkan* cartouche.

8. See *Mingshi*, *juan* 119, p. 3637, and Walton, *Academies and Society in Southern Sung China*, pp. 33–36.

12
Ritual tube (*cong*)
新石器时期或西周　玉琮
Neolithic, ca. 2500 BCE,
    or Western Zhou dynasty (ca. 1050–771 BCE)
Jade
H. 38.2 cm, W. 6.1 cm
The Confucius Museum in Qufu, Shandong Province

Jade *cong* tubes first appeared during the middle of the
Neolithic period in the eastern part of China, where they
were used as ritual objects in burials. The ancient
Chinese held that the earth is square and yellow.
Therefore, it is said in the "Chunguan Dazongbo" chapter
of the *Rites of Zhou*, "Use yellow *cong* tubes to propitiate
the earth."

In the form of a cuboid, the *cong* has a square cross-
section with a hole drilled through the center. This *cong*
tube has thirteen segments. Each segment is carved with
four simplified human-face motifs.

LWS

13
Ritual blade (*chan*)
西周　黄玉铲
Western Zhou dynasty (ca. 1050–771 BCE)
Jade
H. 10.2 cm, W. 5.7 cm
The Confucius Museum in Qufu, Shandong Province
Unearthed from the Cemetery of Confucius,
　Qufu, Shandong

The prototype for this ritual jade blade was the stone shovel. It was a practical tool used for farming during China's Neolithic period that was transformed into a sacrificial object. Called a jade *yue* (battle ax), it became a token of the owner's power of life and death over others. The shovel handle is basically rectangular in shape, while the blade is curved to a slightly upward point at both ends. The top is adorned with a pair of back-turned birds and a hole for passing through a string. The body is carved with an animal-mask motif in low relief.

LWS

14
Ritual disk (*bi*)
战国　玉璧
Warring States period (CA. 475–221 BCE)
Jade
Diam. 19 cm, Thickness 0.8 cm
The Confucius Museum in Qufu, Shandong Province
Excavated in 1978 from Warring States Tomb No. 52 in
　　the ancient capital of Lu state, Qufu, Shandong

Jade disks first appeared during the mid-Neolithic period in the eastern part of China, where they were used as ritual objects in burials. It is said in the "Chunguan Dazongbo" chapter of the *Rites of Zhou* that "celadon jade disks are used to propitiate heaven"; this is because the ancient Chinese thought that the cosmos was round.

"Celadon blue" (*cang*) was also identified as the color of the sky. Therefore, a celadon jade disk was the best choice for ceremonial purposes. This thin, circular disk is decorated with a raised grain pattern and a rib encircling both the outer and inner rims.

LWS

15
Finial for a staff
战国　错金银铜杖首
Warring States period (ca. 475–221 BCE)
Bronze with gold and silver inlay
H. 10 cm, W. 22 cm
The Confucius Museum in Qufu, Shandong Province
Excavated in 1978 from Wangfutai Tomb No. 3 in the
　　ancient capital of Lu state, Qufu, Shandong

Originally used as a walking stick, the staff became a symbol of authority during the late Neolithic period in China. This bronze ornament in the form of several beasts is the finial of a ceremonial staff. The cylindrical opening at the bottom is for installing a cane. Poised atop the cylinder is a large-eyed, dragon-shaped beast with a sloping tail, a contracted body, and a raised head with long jaws. Caught in its jaws is a serpent-bodied creature, looking back and struggling to get free. Coiled atop the dragon-shaped beast is another serpentine creature, shown biting the head of yet another beast, which is in turn holding a bird-tail in its mouth and is attached to the serpentine creature. Fantastically designed with intricate inlays of gold and silver, this staff finial demonstrates superb craftsmanship and distinction of class.

LWS

16
Ornament in eleven pieces
战国　玉佩饰

Warring States period (ca. 475–221 BCE)
Jade
Disk (*bi*): Diam. 5.3 cm
Dragon pendant: W. 11 cm
Elongated drum-shaped tubes: L. 4.5 cm
Beads: Diam. 1 cm
Long pillar tubes: L. 4.5 cm
Short pillar tubes: L. 3.2 cm
Unearthed in 1978 from Qufu, Shandong
Shandong Archeological Research Institute

By the late Neolithic period, jade ornaments were imparted with ritual significance. During the Xia, Shang, and Zhou dynasties, they had become indispensable in ritual music at the altar, in sacrifices to ancestors and the gods, and in a regulated system of insignias. They were also used to distinguish blood relationship and as symbols of social position. Jade accessories are believed to reflect the morals and ethics of the bearer. Confucius had said, "The beauty of jade is reflective of the virtues of a gentleman." He maintained that one could find in jade the following good qualities that one would find in a gentleman: benevolence (*ren*), rectitude (*yi*), respect (*li*), wisdom (*zhi*), trust (*xin*), optimism (*le*), truth (*zhong*), forgiveness (*tian*), confidence (*di*), ambition (*de*), and cultivation (*dao*). In addition to the jade accessories that were made exclusively for wearing, the ancient Chinese also carved jade utensils for daily use.

This finely crafted eleven-piece set includes one jade disk, two drum-shaped tubes, two beads, two long tubes, two short tubes; one carved oblate spheroid, and a single-legged *kui*-dragon pendant.

LWS

17
Graduated set of bells (*bian zhong*)
春秋　铜编钟
Spring and Autumn period (770–ca. 475 BCE)
Bronze
Smallest: H. 12.8 cm, W. 7.5 cm, D. 6 cm
Largest: H. 20.1 cm, W. 14.6 cm, D. 9.5 cm
Shandong Archeological Research Institute
Unearthed in 1977 from Liujiadianzi, Yishui, Shandong

Inscription: 陈大丧史仲高乍铃钟用祈眉寿无疆子子孙孙永宝用之 (*Chen dasangshi Zhong Gao zuo ling zhong yong qi meishou wujiang zi zi sun sun yongbao yong zhi*)

Percussion instruments such as *zhong*, *duo*, and *nao* bells had become institutional for the aristocracy by the Shang dynasty at the latest. Graduated sets of bells emerged during the Western Zhou as important musical equipment, flourished during the Spring and Autumn and Warring States periods, and lasted well into the Qin and Han era. In antiquity, they were made exclusively for rulers and were important as musical accompaniments for singing at sacrifices, imperial appointments of officials, and stately banquets. The tones produced are archaically rich, melodious, and sublime, making the bells especially perfect for accompanying an orchestra. The sound is full of the unique qualities of ancient Chinese music. During the Western Zhou dynasty, a ritual system concerning the size of the bell sets was still being observed. Dukes and nobles could be distinguished by the number of bells, in units of three, that they were qualified to use. Bell sets covering the most comprehensive tonal ranges were only used by the king and his dukes when conducting rituals or entertaining. The term "music from bells and food from bronze" is a reference to the life of a noble.

The nine bells in this set are decorated with coiled serpent motifs and cast in the same shape but in graduated sizes with heights varying from 9 to 20 centimeters. They all bear the same twenty-three-character inscription indicating that this set of instruments was specially made for the use of a certain noble family named Chen.

LWS

18
Set of chimes (*bian qing*)
战国　石编磬
Warring States period (CA. 475–221 BCE)
Limestone
Smallest: H. 10.4 cm, W. 24.7 cm, D. 2.5 cm
　　(Diam. of hole 1.9 cm)
Largest: H. 19.6 cm, W. 55.2 cm, D. 2.6 cm
　　(Diam. of hole 2.5 cm)
Shandong Archeological Research Institute
Unearthed in 1979 from the large Warring States burial
　　site at Dafuguan village in the ancient capital of Qi
　　state, Linzi, Shandong

Qing chimes, fashioned out of stone, are percussion instruments that first appeared in China's late Neolithic period. During the Xia, Shang, and Zhou dynasties, sets of *qing* chimes were used together with graduated bronze bells by kings, dukes, and the aristocracy in ritual ceremonies. A set of stones covering a range of tones is hung in a wooden frame and struck with a mallet to produce music. The instrument was mostly used at court on grand occasions. Lu state was the original producer of stone chimes, and Confucius was actually one of the expert makers of stone chimes during the Spring and Autumn period. This set of eight graduated chimes is made out of a limestone material. The rock deposits along the Si River have been regarded as the best material for chimes.

LWS

19
**Rectangular food container of
    the Earl of Lu (*Lubo xu*)**
西周　铜鲁伯盨
Western Zhou dynasty (ca. 1050–771 BCE)
Bronze
H. 19 cm, W. 35 cm, D. 17 cm
The Confucius Museum in Qufu, Shandong Province
Excavated in 1978 from Wangfutai Tomb No. 48 in the
    ancient capital of Lu state, Qufu, Shandong

The *xu* vessel is a food container of the Western and
Eastern Zhou periods for such grains as rice and
sorghum. A symbol of prestige, it was used as
serviceware together with other bronze vessels such as
the *ding* and the *gui*. This *xu* vessel is rectangular in
shape with rounded corners and a pair of handles on the
sides. It is decorated with a refined pattern of scrolls in a
band along the mouth and foot of the vessel and along
the rim of the lid. The belly section is decorated with a

tile pattern (parallel grooves). The lid is crowned with
four *kui*-dragon plaques and a tiger-shaped knob; its
surface is decorated with the tile pattern and an elephant
trunk motif. Inside the lid is a six-line inscription with a
total of thirty-six characters which basically explains that
this container was made by the Earl of Lu in honor of his
parents and to express his wishes for prosperity and
longevity. The text also serves as evidence that this
vessel had been used by the Earl of Lu.

LWS

20

Covered flask of Mother Hou (*Houmu hu*)
西周　铜侯母壶
Western Zhou dynasty (ca. 1050–771 BCE)
Bronze
H. 38 cm, Diam. 10.2 cm
The Confucius Museum in Qufu, Shandong Province
Excavated in 1978 from Wangfutai Tomb No. 48 in the
　　ancient capital of Lu state, Qufu, Shandong

Inscription: 侯母乍侯父戎壶，用征行，用 求福无疆
　　　　　(*Houmu zuo Houfu ronghu, yong zhengxing,
　　　　　yong qiu fu wujiang*)

The form of this bronze wine flask was derived from the
ceramic jugs of the Neolithic period. Bronze wine flasks like
this one were used by the nobility throughout the Xia,
Shang, and Zhou dynasties. Shaped somewhat like a bullet,
it has a small mouth, a ring foot, and four loop handles
attached to the sides. The two upper loop handles are made
to look like rings held in the mouths of beasts. The vessel
body is decorated with various patterns in four separate
registers. At the top is a row of *kui*-dragons, followed below
by a row of triangles, then elephant-trunk creatures, and
more triangles on the bottom. The ring foot is decorated
with a downward-pointing scale pattern while the lid has a
coiled dragon and two smaller loop handles on its sides.
Along the rim of the lid and around the neck are matching
fifteen-character inscriptions that translate as, "Mother Hou
made this military flask for Father Hou to use on
expeditions and to use for good fortune without end"; it is a
blessing intended for protection, safety, and innumerable
chances of luck when leaving on an expedition of war.

LWS

21
Fragments of the Xiping Stone Classics
东汉　熹平石经残石
Eastern Han dynasty, 175 CE
Stone
(1) H. 14.2 cm, W. 25 cm, D. 10.3 cm
(2) H. 12 cm, W. 13.5 cm, D. 10.6 cm
(3) H. 5.6 cm, W. 0.8 cm, D. 6.5 cm
(4) H. 18.6 cm, W. 0.8 cm, D. 6.5 cm
(5) H. 14 cm, W. 15 cm, D. 6.2 cm
Shandong Provincial Museum
Unearthed from Luoyang, Henan

Commonly known by the name of the era in which it was produced, the Xiping Stone Classics constitute the earliest official set of the Confucian Classics to have been carved onto steles. Due to the uniform style of its clerical-script characters, this group of Han Stone Classics is also known as the Single-Script Stone Classics.

In 175 (4th year of the Xiping reign under Emperor Ling of Han), Imperial Counselor Cai Yong and his supporters petitioned to protect the authenticity of the Six Classics by engraving the texts in stone. The petition was approved by Emperor Ling, and the collated official versions were inscribed onto forty-six steles [in the handwriting of Cai Yong and others] before they were

carved; they were placed in front of the imperial university at Kaiyang Gate in the southern part of the capital city of Luoyang (present-day Zhujiagedang Village, Yanshi, Henan). Each stele measured over one *zhang* (10.9 feet) tall and approximately four *chi* (4.3 feet) wide. Their texts included the *Book of Changes* (*Zhouyi*), the *Classic of History* (*Shangshu*), the *Songs of Lu* (*Lushi*), the *Book of Etiquette and Ceremonial* (*Yili*), the *Spring and Autumn Annals* (*Chunqiu*), the *Commentary of Gongyang* (*Gongyangzhuan*), and the *Analects* (*Lunyu*). Except for the *Analects*, they were all erected by imperial educational institutions. The total character count of the carved books was 200,911. The existence of the Stone Classics had a positive role in correcting far-fetched, biased versions and curbing attempted alterations of the Classics by self-designated scholars. It protected the integrity of the Confucian Classics and provided a standard for students. The Xiping Stone Classics have been held in high esteem for its monumental significance in the history of Chinese ideology, publishing and printing, etymology, and calligraphy. Although the steles had long been destroyed, fragments have been unearthed since Northern Song times. Shown in the current exhibition are five fragments from the steles.

LWS

22

Fragments of the Zhengshi Stone Classics
三国时期（魏国）　正始石经残石
Three Kingdoms period (Wei kingdom), 241 CE
Stone
(1) H. 10.8 cm, W. 7 cm, D. 4.5 cm
(2) H. 6.5 cm, W. 9 cm, D. 4.5 cm
Shandong Provincial Museum
Unearthed from Luoyang, Henan

Known by the era name Zhengshi, this engraving project of the Wei kingdom during the Three Kingdoms period is also known as the Wei Stone Classics or the Three-Script Stone Classics. The engraving was done in 241 (2nd year of the Zhengshi reign), and the tablets were erected west of the imperial university lecture halls in the southern suburbs of the Wei capital Luoyang (present-day Dianzhuang rural district, Yanshi, Henan).

In 220 (1st year of the Huangchu reign under Emperor Wen of Wei), the imperial university was restored and a collation project of the Han Stone Classics was launched. Although only two of the Classics (*Classic of History* and *Spring and Autumn Annals*) were engraved in this project, the new steles were markedly different from their Han predecessors in that they were carved in three different scripts: once in seal script, then in large seal script, and again in clerical script. Therefore, they are also referred to as the Three-Script Stone Classics.

Later during the Northern Dynasties, the Xiping Stone Classics and Zhengshi Stone Classics, the greatest assemblage of Confucian Classics put together in China prior to the Tang dynasty, were to both sustain great damage during several relocations. Because of its presentation in three different scripts, the Zhengshi Stone Classics has been invaluable in the study of and research in Chinese etymology.

Fragments of the Zhengshi Stone Classics have been unearthed from time to time since the late Qing dynasty. In 1922, the largest known fragment came to light at the site of the Luoyang imperial university ruins. On the front face of the fragment are thirty-four lines from two chapters of the *Classic of History*, "Against Luxurious Ease" and "Lord Shi," and on the back side of the fragment are thirty-two lines from the "Duke Xi" chapter of the *Spring and Autumn Annals*, yielding over 1,800 characters of text. In addition to this, there are many more fragments, yielding a total character count of 2,576. Recently, there have been frequent findings of these fragments.

LWS

23
Set of ten Shang and Zhou bronze ritual vessels bestowed by the Qianlong emperor in 1771
乾隆御赐商周十供

Confucius was held in high regard by the Qing dynasty Qianlong emperor, who traveled to Qufu eight times to pay homage to the Sage and wrote many poems in praise of him as a man of "consistent heavenly virtue and a teacher to ancient emperors and kings." On every visit, he made an effort to make his ceremonial presence a grand occasion. Upon his arrival in Qufu, he would go first to the Temple of Confucius to pay homage; on the second day, he would walk all the way to the Hall of Great Accomplishment and perform the utmost salutation of "three kneelings and nine bows" in front of the statue of Confucius. During his third visit, in 1771 (36th year of the Qianlong reign), he personally examined the sacrificial utensils in the temple and was not impressed by what was there; they were, in his words, "just Han manufactures, and the patinas are not that ancient either." To express his reverence for Confucius, he gave orders to "choose ten vessels of the Zhou dynasty from the imperial court collection and have them placed in the hall of the temple, so that the Sage's wishes in following the Zhou rituals can be fulfilled." Upon his return to Beijing, he ordered immediate action to have the ten selected bronze vessels transported to Qufu as a gift to the Kong family. (Actually, some earlier vessels of the Shang dynasty were among the ten chosen.) This was the story of the famous "Ten Shang and Zhou Sacrificial Vessels" (now classified as first class National Cultural Relics). He also issued a special decree to have these vessels placed in the personal care of Kong Zhaohuan, the seventy-first generation Duke for Perpetuating the Sage. In response to the immeasurable imperial favors bestowed upon them, members of the Kong family gave these treasures scrupulous care and would not show them to the public. The only occasions on which these vessels were put to use were during the four annual grand ceremonies (on the *ding* days of the 2nd, 5th, 8th, and 11th months) and on Confucius's birthday; the vessels were placed in front of the statue of Confucius, and after the ceremony they would be promptly removed into storage at the Front Building of the private living quarters inside the Kong Family Mansion. There were several times when the ten vessels had to be removed from the Kong Family Mansion: once in 1885 (11th year of the Guangxu reign), when the Kong Family Mansion suffered a house fire; once during the anti-Japanese War, when Japanese troops had their eyes on the vessels; and during other wars and disorders. The ten vessels returned to the Kong Family Mansion in 1952 and are now preserved in The Confucius Museum.

LWS

23a
Tripod (*Mugong ding*)
商代　铜木工鼎
Shang dynasty (ca. 1600–ca. 1050 BCE)
Bronze (with Qing dynasty wood stand and cover and jade knob)
H. 35.5 cm, W. 25.5 cm, D. 25 cm
The Confucius Museum in Qufu, Shandong Province

Inscription: 作父戊鼎，木工册 (*zuo Fuwu ding, Mugong ce*)

This food container has a flattened lip at the mouth, standing loop handles, slightly convex belly, round bottom, and cylindrical legs. In the decorative zone below the rim are six repeated animal masks, each depicted with curled horns and a protruding flange at the nose ridge. The belly of the vessel is undecorated and smooth. Each leg is adorned with an animal mask and projecting flange. The inner wall of the vessel bears a seven-character inscription in two lines, naming the vessel and its maker. A wooden cover with a jade knob on top, as well as a sandalwood base, was made for it during the Qing. The carved inscription inside the cover reads, "*Qianlong yuzhi*" (from Qianlong's imperial workshop), and the characters on the base read, "*Mugong ding*."

LWS

71

23b
Wine vessel (*gu*)
商代　铜亚弓觚

Shang dynasty (ca. 1600–ca. 1050 BCE)
Bronze (with Qing dynasty wood stand)
H. 32.5 cm, W. (top) 20.5 cm
The Confucius Museum in Qufu, Shandong Province

This *gu* beaker has a wide flaring mouth, a drum-like
body, flat bottom, and a high ring foot. There are
projecting flanges on the body and ring foot. Above the
ring foot are two cross-shaped holes. The belly and the
foot are separated by two circumferential ridges and are
each decorated with animal mask motifs featuring
dimpled bosses as eyes. A red sandalwood stand furnished
during the Qing dynasty bears the carved inscription
"*Qianlong yu shang*" (Qianlong's imperial award); the three
characters "*Zhou ya zun*" are carved on the bottom.

LWS

23c
Covered food-serving vessel (*dou*)
战国　错金银铜夔凤豆

Warring States period (ca. 475–221 BCE)
Bronze inlaid with gold and silver (with Qing dynasty
　　wood stand)
H. 25.2 cm, W. 25.5 cm, D. 19.3 cm
The Confucius Museum in Qufu, Shandong Province

This stemmed *dou* vessel has a bowl-shaped belly with
ear-like loop handles. When covered, the body and lid
form an oblate spheroid. The lid has a large, flaring
circular handle on top that corresponds to the trumpet-
shaped ring foot. The vessel is covered with animal and
bird designs: one-legged, serpentine *kui* dragon and
phoenix motifs on the lid and phoenix and owl motifs on
the bowl. Bits of gold and silver have been inlaid
throughout this design. A red sandalwood stand furnished
during the Qing dynasty is inscribed "*Qianlong yu shang*"
(Qianlong's imperial award); the bottom of the stand is
inscribed "*Zhou kui feng dou.*"

LWS

23d
Square food container (*fangding*)
西周　銅方鼎
Western Zhou dynasty (CA. 1050–771 BCE)
Bronze (with Qing dynasty wood cover and jade knob)
H. 29 cm, W. 27 cm, D. 21 cm
The Confucius Museum in Qufu, Shandong Province

This rectangular container on four hooved legs has a swelling belly, slightly contracted mouth, a flat rim, and a pair of standing loop handles. The upper part of the belly is embellished on all sides with a total of eight raised rectangular frames. A rosewood cover with a jade knob was furnished during the Qing dynasty; it is inscribed "*Qianlong yu shang*" (Qianlong's imperial award) on the inside.

LWS

23e
Wine container (*xizun*)
周代　铜牺尊
Zhou dynasty (ca. 1050–256 BCE)
Bronze (with Qing dynasty carved jade plaque
　　and wood stand)
H. 29 cm, W. 39 cm, D. 15.5 cm
The Confucius Museum in Qufu, Shandong Province

This wine container has a bovine body, back-pointing ears, a short tail, and sturdy legs. Attached to the back of the animal is an oval lid that can be opened. The body is undecorated. A jade plaque carved with a tiger motif in openwork and a rosewood stand was furnished during the Qing dynasty. The stand is inscribed "*Qianlong yu shang*" (Qianlong's imperial award); the bottom of the stand is inscribed "*Zhou xizun*."

LWS

23f
Food-serving vessel (*Boyi gui*)
西周　铜伯彝簋
Western Zhou dynasty (ca. 1050–771 BCE)
Bronze (with Qing dynasty wood base and cover
　　and jade knob)
H. 24.5 cm, W. 29.2 cm, D. 23.1 cm
The Confucius Museum in Qufu, Shandong Province

Inscription: 伯作尊彝用······水······ (*bo zuo zunyi yong...shui...*)

This food-serving vessel is shaped like a drinking cup
with wide mouth, flanged lip, straight-sided body,
rounded bottom, and a slightly splayed ring foot. Each
of the two handles on the sides is in the form of a horned
creature with a hanging tail. The bowl is embellished on
both sides with a raised animal mask above a straight
ridge. On the body are two zones of decorative bands that
form a series of masks with paired eyes set within scrolls
in the upper register and bolder scrolls in the lower half.
The mask of a horned beast is repeated four times around
the ring foot. The inside bottom of the bowl bears a four-
line inscription that has become obscured, leaving only
six legible characters. A sandalwood cover with a jade
knob and a stand were furnished during the Qing
dynasty; the stand bears a four-character inscription
"*Qianlong yu shang*" (Qianlong's imperial award). This
vessel has an elegant shape, distinctive patterns of
decoration, and a beautiful patina.

LWS

23g
Wine container (*Fuyi you*)
商代　铜父乙卣
Shang dynasty (ca. 1600–ca. 1050 BCE)
Bronze
H. 33.5 cm, W. 17.5 cm, D. 24.5 cm
The Confucius Museum in Qufu, Shandong Province

Inscription: 册父乙 (*ce Fuyi*)

This lidded, pear-shaped jug has a slightly contracted
mouth and neck, a drooping belly, and a splayed ring
foot. The fitted, domed lid is topped with a garlic-shaped
knob. A bail handle cast in the form of a rope is attached
at two loops on the shoulder. Except for a nose-like
projecting mask on the shoulder at front and back, the
body is undecorated. The interior bears the inscription
"*ce Fuyi*," matching the one inside the lid.

LWS

23h
Tray (*fu*)
西周　铜宝簠
Western Zhou dynasty (ca. 1050–771 BCE)
Bronze
H. 9.5 cm, W. 34 cm, D. 22 cm
The Confucius Museum in Qufu, Shandong Province

Inscription: □自作□□簠子孙永宝用 (□ *zizuo* □□ *fu, zi sun yongbao yong*)

This rectangular bronze tray has a straight-sided mouth with a flat rim; its sides slope down to a deep bottom. There are a pair of animal-head loop handles on the sides. The square foot around the base has a rectangular cutout on each side. Under the rim, a band of studded scrolls circles the mouth. Beneath that, the walls are decorated with intertwining beasts and eye motifs. The inscription inside the vessel, only part of which is legible, basically means, "for the use of offspring generation after generation."

23i
Covered food-serving vessel (*gui*)
西周　铜蟠夔簋
Western Zhou dynasty (ca. 1050–771 BCE)
Bronze
H. 23.2 cm, W. 27 cm, D. 25.5 cm
The Confucius Museum in Qufu, Shandong Province

This round food-serving vessel features a drum-like belly, a domical fitted lid that serves as a bowl when inverted, and a pair of animal-shaped handles with pendant lugs. The lid is decorated with parallel grooves and a frieze of ribbon-like, coiled *kui*-dragon motifs. The upper part of the pot is decorated with a similar frieze while the lower half is embellished with parallel grooves. The ring foot, which is decorated with a downward-pointing scale pattern, is raised on three zoomorphic feet with animal masks. No inscriptions are found on the vessel. Its greenish patina is exceptionally lustrous.

LWS

23j
Tripod steamer (*yan*)
商代 ／ 西周早期　铜饕餮甗
Shang／early Western Zhou period (16th–11th c. BCE)
Bronze (with Qing dynasty wood cover and jade knob)
H. 42.6 cm, W. 29 cm
The Confucius Museum in Qufu, Shandong Province

This food steamer is a composite of the *zeng* pot and the *li* cauldron. The pot above has a wide mouth, a pair of standing loop handles, a deep belly, and a strainer bottom with cross-shaped openings for steam. Below the rim of the pot is a frieze of ribbon-like spirals around a pair of eyes, forming a stylized mask; the rest of the body is undecorated. The *li* cauldron is sectioned into three connected legs, which are each decorated with an animal mask in relief. A sandalwood cover with a jade knob and a rosewood stand were furnished during the Qing dynasty; the stand is inscribed "*Qianlong yu shang*" (Qianlong's imperial award). This vessel has a beautiful patina and distinctive patterns of decoration.

LWS

24
Box for imperial edicts, bestowed on the Duke for Perpetuating the Sage
清代　御赐封衍圣公奉天诰命金漆木雕盒
Qing dynasty (1644–1911)
Lacquered and gilded carved wood
H. 41.5 cm, W. 45 cm, D. 21 cm
The Confucius Museum in Qufu, Shandong Province

This magnificent wooden box was made to hold the Qing emperor's decrees awarding noble titles to descendants of Confucius (e.g., see cat. no. 25). As early as the Han dynasty, emperors periodically conferred ranks of nobility and material benefits on senior male descendants of Confucius. From 1055 until 1935, the leader in each generation of Kongs was titled Duke for Perpetuating the Sage (*Yanshenggong*). In return for imperial support, the descendants maintained regular sacrifices to Confucius, which were believed to benefit the entire realm. The Manchu rulers of the Qing dynasty enthusiastically continued this mutually beneficial relationship, and the palace maintained frequent contact with the Kong Mansion in Qufu.

Fabricated in a palace workshop, the box displays the familiar imperial symbols of five-clawed dragons cavorting in the clouds over a churning sea. The sides and top of the deep lid are carved all over in fluent high relief, covered with red lacquer and gilt to create a dazzling surface. At the front center of the lid, a hieratic dragon looms over a jewel-topped plaque, which is framed by cloud-spirals and two pairs of rearing dragons in profile. Its inscription is elegantly written in gold on a dark blue ground and reads "By the Command of Heaven" in both Manchu and Chinese (*Fengtian gaoming*), identifying the box as the repository of an imperial edict. Appropriate to the formality of the bequest, the Manchu text is in standard script and the Chinese in small-seal characters. The surrounding decoration visually suggests that the imperial decree is descending from the heavens.

The lower section of the box consists of a recessed rectangular container made of plain hardwood, without nails, which is affixed to a shallow tray on a high, stepped pedestal. A symmetrical pattern of waves adorns the scalloped vertical edges of the tray, and rows of spirals and petals alternate as zones of decoration on the pedestal below. The flange of the lid fits securely between the box and the lip of the tray, creating the appearance of a continuous surface.

JKM

25

Imperial edict conferring a title on the parents of Kong Zhaoqian

清代　御赐孔昭虔父母诰命　卷

Qing dynasty, 1828

Colored inks on patterned silk brocade

33.5 × 384 cm (entire scroll)

The Confucius Museum in Qufu, Shandong Province

Edict title in Manchu (regular script) and Chinese
(seal script): "By the Command of Heaven"
奉天诰命 (*Fengtian gaoming*)

Edict text in Manchu and Chinese (regular script)

Bilingual seal: *Zhigao zhi bao* 制诰之宝 (Daoguang emperor,
r. 1820–50; relief [2 impressions])

During the Qing dynasty, many members of the senior Kong lineage pursued careers in government or distinguished themselves in scholarship, literature, and calligraphy. In this period, it was common for an eminent official to petition the emperor to bestow posthumous honors on his ancestors, particularly ones whose accomplishments may not have been fully recognized in life. Such awards might lead to upgraded burial monuments and new portraits reflecting the higher status, and they reflected favorably on the descendant as well. The impressive document exhibited here grants such honors for Kong Guangsen 孔广森 (1752–1786) and Madame Shen, the deceased parents of Kong Zhaoqian (1775–1835).[1]

The bilingual edict is transcribed in formally written Manchu and Chinese, both of which were official languages during the Qing (Manchu) dynasty. The Chinese version begins at the right with a seal-script title woven into the black silk, reading "By the Command of Heaven" (*Fengtian gaoming*), flanked by a pair of five-clawed vertical dragons. The main text is written in regular script (*kaishu*) on sections of dark grey then red silk brocade. The Manchu version starts at the left with a section of crimson silk containing the title flanked by dragons, then proceeds toward the right through blood-red and cream-colored sections. The brocade is woven throughout with a uniform pattern of *ruyi*-shaped clouds, symbolic of heaven. The two texts meet in the middle on a piece of imperial yellow silk, identifying the recipients once again and giving the date (Daoguang 8/11/9, corresponding to December 15, 1828). Both inscriptions are stamped with the same large imperial seal, which is also bilingual.

A seventy-first-generation descendant and great-grandson of Duke Kong Chuanduo (1674–1735; see cat. no. 28), Kong Zhaoqian passed the *jinshi* examination in 1801 and began his official career as a junior compiler in the prestigious Hanlin Academy.[2] After 1808 he held increasingly elevated provincial posts all over China, including Taiwan, and ended as provincial administration commissioner for Guizhou. Apart from his accomplishments as an official, Kong Zhaoqian was also a scholar of ancient poetry and the author of a couple of plays. In 1828, when he received this edict, he was serving as tax circuit intendant for Jiangxi province. The document mentions his recent promotion to provincial surveillance commissioner for Shaanxi and associated areas.

The main purpose of the edict was to grant the posthumous title of Grand Master Exemplar (*Zhongxian dafu*) to Kong Zhaoqian's father, Kong Guangsen. While just a youth, Kong Guangsen had managed to secure a pardon for his own father, Kong Jifen (1725–1786), who had been sentenced to exile in faraway Yili (Xinjiang).[3] After passing the *jinshi* examination in 1771, Kong Guangsen had entered the Hanlin Academy, but his promising career was cut short by an early death. A number of his writings on ancient ritual and poetry survive.

JKM

1. Kong Zhaoqian's alternate names were (*zi*) Yuanjing and (*hao*) Quanxi. For his biography and publications, see Li Jingming, *Jiazu shixi*, p. 305, and Zhang Yingji, "Kong Zhaoqian zaju 'Tangfu qiu si', 'Sanghua' shangxi."

2. A chronology of Kong Zhaoqian's official career appears at a National Palace Museum website, http://npmhost.npm.gov.tw/ttscgi2/ttsquery?0:0:npmauac:TM%3D%B7q [entry under 第 46 筆] (accessed July 2, 2009).

3. Kong Jifen was a prodigious writer with a great interest in the history of the Kong lineage and the cult of Confucius, and he compiled the encyclopedic *Queli wenxian kao* (1762). However, the Qianlong emperor considered his book on Kong family rites, *Kongshi jiayi*, subversive because it conflicted with the Qing's ritual statutes (*Da Qing huidian*). For a detailed discussion, see Agnew, "Culture and Power," pp. 193 and 203. For Kong Guangsen's role, see Li Jingming, *Jiazu shixi*, p. 302.

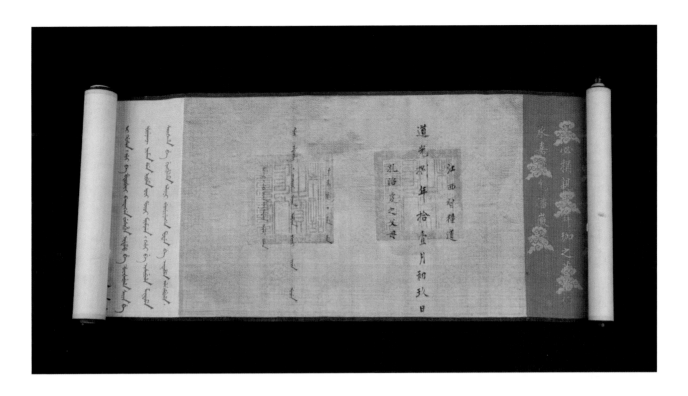

Section with Chinese text

COMMEMORATIVE PORTRAITS OF THE KONG DUKES AND THEIR WIVES

Starting in the Han dynasty, successive emperors awarded ranks of nobility and material emoluments to the senior male in each generation in the direct line of descent from Confucius.[1] From 1055 until 1935, this privileged individual was titled Duke for Perpetuating the Sage (*Yanshenggong*). His chief responsibility was to maintain proper sacrifices to Confucius and to his more immediate ancestors, following the steps prescribed in highly detailed liturgies.[2] By conducting the rites of ancestor worship in exemplary fashion, the Kong descendants embodied the ideals of an ancient ritual system that was associated with Confucius and endorsed by virtually every regime that ruled China.

According to the *Record of Rites* (*Liji*), one of the five "Confucian Classics," a descendant impersonated the dead ancestor during a sacrifice to help the celebrants visualize the spirit receiving offerings of food and wine.[3] After the use of such "personators" (*shi*) was abandoned, painted or sculptural portraits evolved as a substitute means to aid in visualization. Portraits were probably first used in the rites for worshiping imperial ancestors; they then spread to aristocratic families and eventually to other social classes. During the eleventh century, Song ritualists debated the propriety of this nonclassical practice and discussed the qualities necessary for a portrait to serve as an adequate resemblance. According to Cheng Yi (1033–1107), if the representation was not accurate down to the last hair, the sacrifice might go astray.

Memorial portraits

It is unclear when the Kongs in Qufu first began using painted images in sacrifices to their immediate ancestors. Among the thirty-two formal memorial portraits that survive in the collection today, the earliest figure represented is Kong Hongxu (1448–1504), duke of the sixty-first generation.[4] Portraits of an incumbent duke's four predecessors and their wives were hung flanking that of the senior line's founding ancestor, Kong Sihui (1267–1333), during sacrifices in the Hall of Requiting Origins (Baobentang), a family temple inside the eastern part of the Kong Mansion.[5] Paintings were also displayed in the Front Reception Room (Qianshangfang), in the rear section of the Mansion, at the New Year, weddings, and funerals. Multiple portraits were made for some individuals (see cat. no. 26), perhaps to meet needs in separate locations. Also, a duke's posthumous elevation

in rank entitled him and his wives to different emblems on their clothing and thus might require an updated image. And new paintings might be made to replace damaged or old ones. After four generations, portraits, spirit tablets, and ritual vessels were stored in the Memorial Temple (Tiaomiao) behind and north of the Hall of Requiting Origins.[6]

Portraits intended for use in memorial rites follow a set of standard conventions, and much of the picture could be prepared ahead of time. A proper portrait represented the individual's social identity as well as idiosyncratic physical appearance. The sitter appears in formal costume decorated with emblems appropriate to his or her rank, often featuring an animal- or bird-themed rank badge on the chest, and wearing an elaborate headdress.[7] Positioned in a fully frontal view, the figure is seated in a fabric-draped armchair on a brightly colored carpet, which is typically decorated with geometric designs and sometimes auspicious flowers, especially peonies. Often the sitter's body virtually disappears amid this riot of ornament, and his or her face seems awkwardly balanced at its apex. Although depicted as if sitting for his or her portrait, the subject did not "model" for it and was not present when it was painted. The chair, carpet, and other elements of the setting were conventional motifs, probably invented by the painting workshop, rather than depictions of real furnishings.

The face was the only part of a memorial portrait that was expected to capture the individual's likeness.[8] A skilled specialist might be engaged to add it, perhaps based on sketches he made from personal observation or from description by family members. Nonetheless, certain facial features may be exaggerated to conform with enduring beliefs about correlations between physical appearance, inborn character, and destiny.[9] Texts on physiognomy (*xiangshu*) going back to the Han period led portraitists to treat the face as a cosmic diagram in which every feature had significance. For example, high cheekbones were a sign of authority and big ears signaled wisdom (e.g., cat. nos. 26 and 28). By the late Ming, woodblock-printed illustrated manuals that codified facial attributes and their explanations provided portraitists with a handy reference.

Although the sitter's eyes look directly out from a memorial painting, they do not fully engage the viewer, and the face displays no emotion. The impassive, remote expression aptly symbolizes the liminal state in which ancestors are thought to exist. Although physically gone from the world, their spirits still linger, able to come and enjoy the offerings of their descendants and influence their fortunes. The introduction of photography during the nineteenth century led some portraitists to copy the faces for memorial paintings from photographs, resulting in greater expressiveness (e.g., cat. no. 30). In such portraits, the startling verisimilitude of the face contrasts sharply with the conventional treatment of the rest of the figure.

Other kinds of portraits

In addition to the formal memorial portraits of the dukes and their wives, fifteen assorted other paintings in the Kong Mansion's collection were made for more informal kinds of remembrance.[10] Two are half-length or "bust" portraits (called *yunshen xiang*) in which the representation closely resembles the upper part of a memorial image. Nine paintings that depict a standing figure or a sitter surrounded by objects that suggest his or her interests and personality (e.g., cat. no. 27) are called "small" or "minor" portraits (*xiao xiang*), regardless of their size. Finally, four "pursuing pleasure" portraits (*xingle xiang*) show a man enjoying his pastimes outdoors in a landscape setting. Even when portrayed in an anecdotal environment and wearing clothing suggestive of leisure, however, the sitter typically displays a stiff, formal posture and expressionless face, resulting in a representation that is timeless and symbolic.

The five paintings in this part of the exhibition have been selected to suggest the variety of portraits extant today in the collection of the Kong Mansion. They include three formal portraits of dukes: one from the late Ming period (cat. no. 26), one from the mid-Qing (cat. no. 28), and one from the Republican period (cat. no. 30). The two paintings that depict women include an informal "small portrait" of the late Ming duke's first wife (cat. no. 27) and a Qing memorial portrait of the mid-Qing duke's second wife (cat. no. 29)

JKM

1. For a history of the Kong lineage and biographies of its dukes, see Li Jingming, *Jiazu shixi*.

2. For a vivid recreation of such ceremonies, see Nylan and Wilson, *Lives of Confucius*, chap. 6.

3. See detailed discussions in Sommer, "Destroying Confucius," pp. 97–103, and Stuart and Rawski, *Worshiping the Ancestors*, chap. 1.

4. See *Kongzi xiang, Yanshenggong ji furen xiaoxiang*, pp. 13–16.

5. Kong Sihui was the 54th-generation descendant given the ducal title in 1316. Spirit tablets inscribed with names and titles accompanied the painted portraits inside the 5-bay hall. Sacrifices were offered on the birth and death days of those enshrined; see *Kongzi xiang, Yanshenggong ji furen xiaoxiang*, pp. 13–16. Thomas Wilson provides a detailed description of the setting and the liturgy of a sacrifice performed at the winter solstice in 1746; see Nylan and Wilson, *Lives of Confucius*, chap. 6.

6. Kong Jifen, *Kongshi jiayi ji, juan* 1, pp. 367–68, quoted in Agnew, "Culture and Power," p. 202.

7. For a guide to robe emblems, see Garrett, *Chinese Dress*; also Stuart and Rawski, *Worshiping the Ancestors*, chap. 2.

8. See Stuart and Rawski, *Worshiping the Ancestors*, chap. 3.

9. See Siggstedt, "Forms of Fate."

10. See *Kongzi xiang, Yanshenggong ji furen xiaoxiang*, pp. 13–16, and individual reproductions in the plates section.

26

Anonymous

Memorial Portrait of Kong Shangxian, 64th-generation Duke for Perpetuating the Sage
明代　六十四代衍圣公孔尚贤衣冠像　立轴

Ming dynasty, ca. 1622
Hanging scroll; ink and color on silk
200 × 122.5 cm (painting only)
303 × 144.5 cm (overall with mounting)
The Confucius Museum in Qufu, Shandong Province

Kong Shangxian (1544–1622) became the senior descendant of Confucius after his father's death in 1556 but was officially installed as duke only in 1559, after being educated at the imperial university in Beijing.[1] Serving five Ming emperors during his unusually long tenure, he made many visits to Beijing. When he passed away on one such visit at the age of seventy-eight, the Tianqi emperor (r. 1620–27) made lavish provisions for his return to Qufu and burial in the Kong Cemetery. In 1628 the Chongzhen emperor (r. 1627–44) awarded him the posthumous rank of Senior Guardian of the Heir Apparent (*Taizi taibao*).[2] Under the Qing dynasty, he was raised further to Grand Master for Splendid Happiness (*Guanglu dafu*).

Carefully painted on pale gold silk, the portrait shows Kong Shangxian in the formal attire of a Ming official, wearing a stiff-eared black gauze cap and a crimson robe ornamented with cloud-swirl patterns and large rank badge depicting a four-clawed *mang* dragon. The dragon also appears on the white plaques (intended to suggest jade) of his large belt, another attribute of his rank. He sits on a yoke-backed armchair of brown and black *tixi* lacquer, carved in pommel-scroll designs and draped with a gold-on-blue textile. Behind him at the (viewer's) right is a round black-lacquer table with mother-of-pearl inlay, convex legs, and an inset marble top. On it are a bronze tripod ornamented with the Eight Trigrams (*bagua*) and lion-shaped knob, a bamboo container for incense, and a narrow-necked bronze vase with a dragon crawling in relief, containing a piece of coral, a peacock feather, and a branch of flowering cassia.

This painting is the less ornate of two surviving full-length portraits of Kong Shangxian, the other of which bears several inscriptions and probably served as his official memorial portrait during the Qing period.[3] It shows him as somewhat older, with a gaunt face and white hair, and wearing a more fully embellished costume. The table, moreover, is larger and rectangular, and it supports a vase with two peacock feathers, suggesting his posthumous promotion.

A third extant portrait is a bust-length painting of Kong Shangxian, labeled along the right edge with just his Ming posthumous title and called a "legacy portrait" (*yixiang*).[4] It displays the same robe as depicted in the version exhibited here, but its sitter has the gaunter face of the more elaborate portrait.

JKM

1. See his biography in Li Jingming, *Jiazu shixi*, pp. 258–61. His alternate names were (*zi*) Xiangzhi and (*hao*) Xi'an and Longyu.
2. The scroll containing the Chongzhen emperor's handwritten edict conferring posthumous titles on Duke Kong Shangxian and Madame Zhang, the birth-mother of his successor, Kong Yinzhi (1592–1648), is extant and reproduced in *Qufu: Kongzi de guxiang*, plate 90; see also *Da zai Kongzi*, p. 100.
3. *Kongzi xiang, Yanshenggong ji furen xiaoxiang*, pp. 13–14, 16, and 20. The inscriptions were apparently added during inventories of the portraits. The earliest one on Kong Shangxian's portrait, added between 1644 and 1668, is a simple notation in four regular-script characters along the upper left edge, identifying his generation. The second, datable between 1718 and 1722, appears in a column slightly to the right and gives his generation, ducal title, taboo name, and alternate names. The third, written in small-seal script by Hu Erle between 1735 and 1743, is a large title across the top of the painting giving Kong Shangxian's added titles and posthumous honors in addition to his generation, ducal title, and *hao*.
4. See *Kongzi xiang, Yanshenggong ji furen xiaoxiang*, pp. 14, 16, and 22. The unsigned note was written in the Daoguang era (1821–50) by Feng Yunpeng (active ca. 1720–after 1752), a secretary in the Grand Secretariat.

27

Anonymous

Portrait of Madame Yan, Wife of Kong Shangxian, 64th-generation Duke for Perpetuating the Sage

明代　六十四代衍圣公诰命严夫人肖像　立轴

Ming dynasty (1368–1644)
Hanging scroll; ink and color on silk
187 × 101 cm (painting only)
343.5 × 129 cm (overall with mounting)
The Confucius Museum in Qufu, Shandong Province

Madame Yan (1547–1602) was the first wife of Kong Shangxian (1544–1622), the sixty-fourth-generation Duke for Perpetuating the Sage (see cat. no. 26). A native of Fenyi, Jiangxi, she came from a powerful family with whom the Kong lineage had longstanding connections.[1] Her grandfather Yan Song (1481–1565) and father Yan Shifan (1513–1565) dominated the Ming central government in the mid-sixteenth century.[2] Madame Yan's marriage must have occurred before 1565, when they fell spectacularly from favor and the family's immense wealth was confiscated. She did not produce an heir.

Perhaps something of the Yan family's tradition of interest in the arts is conveyed in this painting, which is classed as a "small portrait" and was not used in memorial sacrifices. Sitting primly with her hands concealed inside her sleeves, Madame Yan appears as the refined and cultivated matron of an aristocratic household. The elegantly appointed studio suggests the pleasures of her daily life. A book, scissors, and a ruler rest beside her on the couch, and a tastefully monochrome tree-and-rock painting hangs on the wall behind her. In the foreground, a large ceramic pot of orchids on a red stand echoes the flowering peonies in her garden, visible through the moon window.

Great care is lavished on material details in this large and dramatic painting. The aristocratic floral theme is continued in the colorful scrolling-peony pattern on the silk cushion of her broad couch, whose back displays open fretwork. Dragons and flaming pearls adorn her garments, indicating the high rank she enjoyed as the duke's wife. A four-clawed gold-and-silver dragon cavorts over her dark blue cloak, thrown casually on the couch, and her skirt displays a roundel with another four-clawed dragon rearing over mountains and waves. Her fur-lined pale blue surcoat is covered with a barely perceptible pattern of dragons, pearls, and clouds, suggesting a brocade of the highest quality. A jewel-encrusted triangular cloth on her forehead complements her earrings of gold, pearl, and precious stones. A multilobed collar of red petals fastened with a gold clasp completes her outfit.

JKM

1. In 1546 Yan Song provided monumental seal-script calligraphy to be incised on the grave stele of the 62nd-generation duke, Kong Wenshao (1482–1548); see reproduction in Gu Chuanxiang, *Qufu luyou daguan*, p. 46.
2. See *Dictionary of Ming Biography*, pp. 1586–91.

28

Anonymous

Memorial Portrait of Kong Chuanduo, 68th-generation Duke for Perpetuating the Sage

清代　六十八代衍圣公孔传铎衣冠像　立轴

Qing dynasty (1644–1911)

Hanging scroll; ink and color on silk

186.5 × 100 cm (painting only)

246.5 × 131 cm (overall with mounting)

The Confucius Museum in Qufu, Shandong Province

Title in large characters of small-seal script, by Hu Erle (active ca. 1720–after 1752): "Legacy Portrait of Duke Zhenlu, Hereditary Duke for Perpetuating the Sage in the 68th Generation, with Added Title Grand Master for Splendid Happiness, Conferred by the Imperial Qing" (*Huang Qing gao zeng Guanglu dafu liushiba dai gongfeng Yanshenggong Zhenlu gong yixiang* 皇清诰赠光禄大夫六十八代供奉衍圣公振路公遗像)

Inscription on lower left edge: "Respectfully inscribed in seal script by Hu Erle, the later scholar of Jiangzuo [Jiangsu]" (*Jiangzuo houxue Hu Erle jing ti bing zhuan* 江左後学胡二乐敬题并篆).

Seals on lower left edge:

Hu Erle 胡二乐 (Hu Erle; relief)

Xiangxu 象虚 (Hu Erle; relief)

As the eldest son and heir of Duke Kong Yuqi (1656–1723), Kong Chuanduo (1674–1735) received the title Hanlin Erudite of the Five Classics (*Hanlin Wujing boshi*) in 1701, along with the award of second-rank court robes.[1] For several years before his formal accession in 1724, he substituted for his ailing father at sacrifices. He himself suffered from arthritis, and the Yongzheng emperor (r. 1723–35) transferred his ritual responsibilities in Beijing to his second son, Kong Jipu (b. ca. 1700), since the eldest (by Madame Li; see cat. no. 29) had already died.

Shortly after Kong Chuanduo became duke, a great fire devastated the major buildings of the Qufu temple. Although he was able to rescue the spirit tablets of Confucius and the other sixteen men enshrined in the Hall of Great Accomplishment, the building was completely destroyed. Between 1724 and 1730, Kong Chuanduo oversaw the massive project to reconstruct the temple and enjoyed generous support from the Yongzheng emperor, who sent artisans from the palace workshops to assist. The buildings were enlarged and given yellow-tile roofs, attaining a grandeur comparable to that of the imperial palace.

The seal-script title across the top of his memorial portrait was written by Hu Erle, a scholar who came to Qufu in 1730 to help compile *Grand Ceremonials of Queli* (*Queli shengdian*), documenting the newly rebuilt temple.[2] Hu also wrote title inscriptions on fifteen memorial portraits, of which Kong Chuanduo's is the latest. In 1731, due to illness, Kong Chuanduo withdrew from the ducal office entirely and was succeeded by his grandson Kong Guangqi (1713–1743). He wrote commentaries on the *Classic of Rites* and was also an accomplished poet.[3]

Kong Chuanduo's portrait displays meticulous attention to the sumptuous materials and patterns of his attire and surroundings. Over a blue court robe adorned with golden five-clawed dragons above mountains and waves, he wears a black or dark purple gauze summer surcoat, emblazoned with a square rank badge divided in two and buttoned down the center. His sleeves, collar, and skirt are trimmed with gold-on-black brocade borders. A finial with ruby and pearls guarded by golden dragons surmounts his court hat, which is covered with red silk floss and lined with gold-on-red brocade. With his right hand, he fingers a bead of his coral and jade court necklace (cf. cat. no. 38). A green textile with red floral designs covers his armchair and much of the intricately patterned stool, which rests on a colorful carpet.

JKM

1. For biographical information, see Li Jingming, *Jiazu shixi*, pp. 287–91; *Kongzi xiang, Yanshenggong ji furen xiaoxiang*, p. 43; or *Kongzi shijia pu*, juan 3, part 1, p. 23a-b (107). His alternate names were (*zi*) Zhenlu and (*hao*) Yongmin.

2. *Kongzi xiang, Yanshenggong ji furen xiaoxiang*, pp. 14 and 16. At the time, Hu Erle (*zi*, Xiangyu) was a stipend student (*linsheng*); he later passed the provincial *juren* examination. His signature identifies him as a native of Shexian, in modern Anhui.

3. For titles and information on these and other writings by Kong Chuanduo, see Li Jingming, *Jiazu shixi*, p. 290.

29

Anonymous

Memorial Portrait of Madame Li, Wife of Kong Chuanduo, 68th-generation Duke for Perpetuating the Sage

清代　六十八代衍圣公继配李夫人衣冠像　立轴

Qing dynasty (1644–1911)

Hanging scroll; ink and color on silk

176.5 × 97 cm (painting only)

313.5 × 118 cm (overall with mounting)

The Confucius Museum in Qufu, Shandong Province

Madame Li Yu (1675–1714) was the second wife of Duke Kong Chuanduo (1674–1735; see cat. no. 28) and the mother of his eldest son and heir, Kong Jihuo (1697–1719), who died before he could accede to the ducal title.[1] The daughter of Li Jiong (1620–1695), vice minister of the Board of Punishment, she came from Shouguang, Shandong. Local tradition in her hometown claims that she did not have bound feet, unusual for a Han woman of the upper class.[2]

This large portrait devotes meticulous detail to Madame Li's sumptuous outfit. On her head she wears a gold and kingfisher crown decorated with openwork phoenixes, accented with rubies, and bordered below with a row of pearls. Suspended on each side are two pairs of long gold pendants, strung with pearls and rubies, which match her earrings and brooch. Her red robe displays golden four-clawed *mang* dragons and multicolored *ruyi* cloud patterns. A belt with inset plaques of white jade, carved with dragons in relief,

secures the garment over a frontal dragon. The lower portion of the robe and the skirt under it display stylized and colorful mountains, waves, and flaming jewels rendered in two different styles.

Somewhat incongruously for such a finely detailed painting, the garment folds are roughly rendered in broad purplish streaks simply overlaid on the textile patterns, without suggesting volume. This schematic treatment also contrasts with the naturalistic rendering of her delicate facial features, which are softly tinged with pale red pigment. Meticulous attention is also given to the furnishings, down to the wood grain and metal fittings of her yoke-backed armchair and stool. The green textile covering her chair displays a pattern of tiny dragons inside octagonal frames. The carpet features large pink peonies and curling green vines on a white background; white raindrop-like highlights add texture to the surface.

A second painting in the Kong Mansion collection is also identified as a memorial portrait of Madame Li, but it seems to depict a woman considerably older than thirty-nine, the age at which she passed away.[3] The bud-like mouth and pointed oval of her dainty face here also differ from the older woman's portrait.

JKM

1. Kong Jihuo gained the ducal title posthumously in 1735, after his father's death, and his son Guangqi (1713–1743) became the next duke. For their memorial portraits see *Kongzi xiang, Yanshenggong ji furen xiaoxiang*, pp. 46, 48–49.
2. This story and others about Madame Li are discussed in Qiu Jiaxing, "Shouguang shengren mu."
3. *Kongzi xiang, Yanshenggong ji furen xiaoxiang*, plate 44.

CONFUCIUS: HIS LIFE AND LEGACY IN ART

30

Anonymous

Memorial Portrait of Kong Lingyi, 76th-generation Duke for Perpetuating the Sage

民国　七十六代衍圣公孔令贻衣冠像　立轴

Republic, ca. 1919

Hanging scroll; ink and color on paper

201 × 95 cm (painting only)

374 × 124 cm (overall with mounting)

The Confucius Museum in Qufu, Shandong Province

Kong Lingyi (1872–1919) acceded to the ducal title in 1877 as a young child and assumed its full duties only in 1889, after an audience with the Guangxu emperor (r. 1875–1908) in 1888.[1] On that occasion, the emperor bestowed large characters reading "Good Fortune" (*fu*) and "Longevity" (*shou*) in his own calligraphy, which are still displayed in the Kong Mansion. Another of Kong Lingyi's many visits to Beijing was for Empress Dowager Cixi's sixtieth birthday celebration in 1894 (see cat. no. 34). Throughout his life, he maintained close relations with the Qing imperial family and court, even after the 1911 revolution. In 1917 he supported the short-lived restoration of the deposed child-emperor Pu Yi (1906–1967) to the throne.[2] He died in Beijing on one of his many visits.

Although the 1911 revolution temporarily abolished sacrifices to Confucius, President Yuan Shikai (1859–1916) restored them in 1913 with Kong Lingyi's assistance. When Yuan proclaimed himself emperor in 1916, he awarded Kong Lingyi the additional title of Commandery Prince (*junwang*). After Yuan's death, Kang Youwei (1858–1927) called for Confucianism to be established as China's religion, and Kong Lingyi circulated a telegram supporting the proposal, which ultimately proved unsuccessful. During his tenure as duke, Kong Lingyi presided over three periods of restoration and rebuilding at the Qufu temple, in 1897, 1908, and 1915. In 1904 he succeeded in having a planned railway line redirected away from the Kong Cemetery to avoid disturbing the spirits of Confucius and his descendants.

Kong Lingyi posed for numerous photographs during his life, and one served as a model for the face in his memorial portrait. The painting accordingly displays a heightened contrast between his naturalistically rendered features and the stylized setting. No longer a novelty by 1919, photographic effects were appreciated for the realism with which they evoked a deceased ancestor.

The painting embodies Kong Lingyi's loyalty to the deposed Qing dynasty by depicting him in formal court costume. He wears a sable surcoat, reserved for Qing nobility, which is ornamented with leaf-shaped tufts of white fur from the animal's neck.[3] The visible portions of his skirt and sleeves feature golden five-clawed dragons contending for a flaming jewel amid colored clouds over mountain peaks rising from the waves. His sable-rimmed court hat is topped with a ruby. With his left hand, he fingers his court necklace (cf. cat. no. 38), whose individual beads of coral, jade, and other precious stones are dotted with white to indicate light reflections.

A tiger skin, complete with paws, covers most of the yoke-back armchair and footrest, whose black-lacquered surfaces are richly ornamented with gilded floral motifs and squared spiral designs. The exuberant carpet design features large, brightly colored peonies linked by vines, creating a curvilinear momentum that contrasts with the angular energy of the geometric motif under the chair.

JKM

1. For biographical information, see Li Jingming, *Jiazu shixi*, pp. 336–42, and *Kongzi xiang, Yanshenggong ji furen xiaoxiang*, p. 58. His alternate names were (*zi*) Gusun and (*hao*) Yanting.

2. Engineered by the warlord-general Zhang Xun (1854–1923), the restoration lasted less than three weeks. Kong Lingyi sent multiple telegrams of congratulations and donated funds to erect a Living Shrine for Zhang in Qufu; Li Jingming, *Jiazu shixi*, p. 340. His daughter, Kong Demao, claims that he and Zhang were sworn brothers in her "Kongfu neizhai yishi," p. 168.

3. He undoubtedly wore it when he attended Pu Yi's birthday celebration in 1919, described by Reginald Johnston, at which men who had been granted the right to wear the sable surcoat displayed them; cited in Dickinson and Wrigglesworth, *Imperial Wardrobe*, pp. 116 and 118.

31

Official seals of the Duke for Perpetuating the Sage

清代　衍圣公木印一组

Qing dynasty (1644–1911)
Wood
Shandong Provincial Museum
Ex collection Kong Family Mansion

From left to right:

A. *Changyuanxian fengsiguan qianji*
长垣县奉祀官钤记
H. 3.6 cm, W. 6.2 cm, D. 6.2 cm

This seal is shaped like an inverted peck-measure (truncated pyramid) with no knob. The legend is carved in relief on the underside. It is the seal of a county-level official in charge of sacrificial offerings to Confucius.

B. *Zhisheng fengsiguan fu sitian guanli chu tuji*
至圣奉祀官府祀田管理处图记
H. 3.6 cm, W. 5.5 cm, D. 5.5 cm

This seal is also shaped like an inverted peck-measure with no knob. The twelve-character seal-script legend is carved in relief. It is the official seal for the management of the Kong family estate land in Qufu for sacrificial purposes.

C. *Yanshenggong yin*
衍圣公印
H. 11 cm, W. 5.8 cm, D. 5.6 cm

This seal has a peg handle on top. The four-character regular-script legend, carved in relief, translates as "Seal of the Duke for Perpetuating the Sage." It was the official seal used exclusively by the eldest lineal male descendant of Confucius in the Kong family.

LWS

32
Private seal of 74th-generation
Kong descendant
清代孔子七十四代孙水晶私印（复制品）
Qing dynasty, 19th century (replica)
Crystal
H. 12.5 cm, W. 7.5 cm
Shandong Provincial Museum
Ex collection Kong Family Mansion

Legend: *Kongzi qishisi dai sun Fanhao zhiyin*
孔子七十四代孙繁灏之印

This charming crystal seal with a handle in the shape of
a lion belonged to Kong Fanhao (1806–1862), who was, as
indicated by the eleven-character legend carved in relief,
a seventy-fourth-generation descendant of Confucius. |
As senior male member of the family, he was in fact the
seventy-fourth-generation Duke for Perpetuating the Sage
mentioned in a colophon on the *Portrait of Confucius as
Minister of Justice in Lu* (cat. no. 1). Carved with his name,
such a seal was more likely used for personal communication or on works in his collection rather than official
business pertaining to his rank.

33

Official robe of the Duke for
   Perpetuating the Sage

明代　衍圣公香色麻飞鱼官服

Ming dynasty (1368–1644)
Linen and silk
135 x 250 cm
Shandong Provincial Museum
Ex collection Kong Family Mansion

Featuring an overlapping lapel opening to the right, loose sleeves, and a gathered waist, this incense-colored robe is tailored in the *yisan* style.* The neck is finished with a trim of white silk. A colorful design of waves against cliffs and fish is woven on the chest and back. The shoulders, sleeves, and lower half of the skirt are embellished with

flying fish amidst clouds. The flying-fish robe was a kind of gift apparel bestowed by emperors of the Ming dynasty.

LWS

* A long garment with large skirt-like pleats in the front and a straight piece in the back (translator's note).

34

Empress Dowager Cixi (1840–1908)

Pine and Crane (Longevity Painting), bestowed
    by Empress Dowager Cixi on Madame Peng,
    Mother of Duke Kong Lingyi

清代　慈禧太后赐彭夫人松鹤图　立轴

Qing dynasty, 1894

Hanging scroll; gold pigment on paper

115 × 55 cm (painting only)

248 × 76.5 cm (overall with mounting)

The Confucius Museum in Qufu, Shandong Province

Inscription in gold ink in upper right, Empress Dowager
    Cixi: "Written by the imperial brush in the autumn of
    [1894]" (*Guangxu jiawu nian qiu xiahuan yubi*
    光绪甲午年秋下浣御笔)

Inscription in gold ink in lower left, a quatrain of poetry in
    lines of seven characters each, "reverently inscribed" by
    Wang Yirong 王懿荣

Colophon on the mounting (half on the right and half on the
    left of the painting) by Kong Lingyi

    (right side): "The imperial brush of Empress Dowager
    Cixi... [November 2, 1894]" (*Cixi Duanyou Kangyi Zhaoyu
    Zhuangcheng Shougong Qinxian Chongxi Huang taihou
    yubi, Guangxu ershi nian shi yue chu wu ri*
    慈禧端佑康颐昭豫庄诚寿恭钦献崇熙皇太后御笔，
    光绪二十年十月初五日)

    (left side): "Conferred title of ducal lady, first class, on
    Madame Peng, mother of servitor Kong Lingyi, Hereditary
    Duke for Perpetuating the Sage" (*Gongfeng Yanshenggong
    chen Kong Lingyi zhi mu gaofeng yipin gong furen Peng shi*
    袭封衍圣公臣孔令贻之母诰封一品公夫人彭氏)

Seals (upper right):

    Daya zhai 大雅斋

    (Empress Dowager Cixi; relief)

    Jing rong zhu he 镜荣烛和

    (Empress Dowager Cixi; relief)

    Yong shou le kai 永寿乐恺

    (Empress Dowager Cixi; relief)

Seals (upper center):

    Cixi huang taihou zhi bao 慈禧皇太后之宝

    (Empress Dowager Cixi; relief)

Seals (lower left):

    Fa tian li dao 法天立道

    (Wang Yirong; relief)

    Hanlin gongfeng 翰林供奉

    (Wang Yirong; intaglio)

Empress Dowager Cixi personally bestowed this painting of a crane flying over the boughs of a pine tree on Madame Peng (1849–1908), the widow of the seventy-fifth-generation Duke for Perpetuating the Sage, Kong Xiangke (1848–1876), and mother of his successor, Kong Lingyi (1872–1919, the 76th-generation Duke for Perpetuating the Sage; see cat. 30). Madame Peng herself came from an illustrious Suzhou lineage of officials, and her grandfather Peng Yunzhang (1792–1862) had been a grand secretary.[1] In the autumn of 1894, she accompanied Duke Kong Lingyi and his wife to Beijing for the empress dowager's sixtieth birthday celebrations. Invited to stay in a wing of the imperial palace, the party socialized with Cixi and enjoyed calligraphy with her.[2]

For centuries, the motifs of crane and pine have served to convey wishes for the recipient's longevity in poetry as well as the visual arts, making them suitable subjects for gifts to someone who was at least middle-aged. Although Madame Peng was actually several years younger than the empress dowager, her position in the lineage of Confucius's descendants led Cixi to treat her with respect. Conversely, the empress-dowager's favor also enhanced the prestige of the Kong family, and her bequests of calligraphy and painting were subsequently carved on stone tablets for display in the Kong Mansion.[3]

Cixi entered the palace from the Yehenala clan of the Manchu Bordered-Blue Banner in 1851 as a concubine of the Xianfeng emperor (r. 1850–61). Quickly rising in favor and rank, she later became a regent for her son, the

Tongzhi emperor (r. 1861–74), and then her nephew, the Guangxu emperor (r. 1875–1908). She wielded considerable power in political affairs, usually working through trusted court officials.

Generally conservative in her support of traditional practices of all kinds, the empress dowager followed time-honored precedents for bestowing calligraphy and painting on chosen recipients and typically chose auspicious motifs as her subjects. Although she did the paintings herself on occasion, scrolls ghostpainted for her by court artists are far more numerous among her gifts to others.[4] However, during the period between 1889 and 1898, Cixi was temporarily retired as regent and had more time for the arts. She recruited a number of gifted female artists who guided her practice of painting and calligraphy and may well have produced most of this work herself.[5]

The configuration of *Pine and Crane* follows Cixi's typical format, which Kabo Tsang has described as follows: "The compositional elements would be disposed to the lower two-thirds of the painting proper; a large square seal with the legend *Cixi huangtaihou zhi bao* (a treasure of the Empress Dowager Cixi) would be impressed at the center just below the upper border; a short dated inscription claiming the work to have been from the imperial brush, followed by one or two of Cixi's supplementary seals, would be located to either the left- or right-hand side in the upper third of the painting proper; and a laudatory poem or two composed by one or more high officials with both literary and calligraphic skills would be written in spaces specifically reserved for this purpose in the lower half."[6]

This work stands out from others in its use of gold ink on dark blue paper, a technique that has strong associations with paintings of Buddhist divinities and perhaps conferred greater efficacy on the visual emblems of longevity. Besides gold, some silver pigment is also used on the pine, whose needles spray out from the clawlike twigs in pale, symmetrical clusters. The sinuous branches are firmly drawn in gold, accented with dots of silver that have oxidized to grey.

The poem at lower left was written by Wang Yirong (1845–1900), a *jinshi* of 1880 and an eminent literatus in the prestigious Hanlin Academy. Cixi greatly admired his calligraphy and poetry, and his inscriptions appear on a number of works that she bestowed on favored subjects.

JKM

1. See his biography in *Eminent Chinese of the Ch'ing Period*, pp. 620–21.
2. See Kong Demao, "Kongjia neizhai yishi," p. 163. In the course of the visit, Cixi also wrote the character for "Longevity" (*shou*) in large regular-script calligraphy for Madame Peng and another in more cursive script for the duke; reproduced in *Qufu: Kongzi de guxiang*, plate 79, and *Da zai Kongzi*, p. 99.
3. See photograph in *Tianxia diyi jia*, p. 167.
4. Tsang, "In Her Majesty's Service," pp. 36–37.
5. Ibid.; also Weidner [Haufler] et al., *Views from Jade Terrace*, p. 159.
6. Tsang, "In Her Majesty's Service," p. 45.

35

"Imperially bestowed 'Poetry, Documents, Ritual, Music'" seal

明代　御赐 "诗书礼乐" 黑寿山石印

Ming dynasty (1368–1644)
Soapstone (*shoushan shi*)
H. 7.2 cm, W. 6 cm, D. 3.5 cm
The Confucius Museum in Qufu, Shandong Province

Legend: *Yuci shi shu li yue*
御赐诗书礼乐

Carved from an irregularly shaped piece of dark brown soapstone, the upper part of this seal depicts a three-dimensional mountain landscape in miniature. Under swirling clouds, four men are boating past a cliff with overhanging trees. The scene may refer to the Song poet Su Shi's (1037–1101) visit to the Red Cliff (Chibi), site of a third-century battle during the Three Kingdoms period. Su's famous poems on the subject became a popular theme for illustration in Ming paintings, woodblock prints, and objects for the scholar's desk.[1]

The underside of the seal displays the six characters *yu ci shi, shu, li, yue*, or "imperially bestowed 'Poetry, Documents, Ritual, Music,'" referring to four of the classic texts that Confucius was believed to have edited. The entire design is enclosed within a pair of sinuous *kui* dragons, symbolizing the emperor. The dragons and two-character, clerical-script (*li shu*) heading are carved intaglio and appear in reserve in the seal impression. The other four characters, written in slightly larger seal script (*zhuan shu*), were left in relief when the surrounding rectangular panel was carved away, so the lines print in red.

JKM

1. For translations, see *Selected Poems of Su Tung-p'o*, pp. 94–98; for selected artworks on the theme, see *Chibi fu shuhua tezhan*.

36
Set of five altar vessels
清代　画珐琅五供

Qing dynasty (1644–1911)
Painted enamel and gilt copper
Incense burner: H. 70.5 cm, W. (including handles) 65 cm
Vases (2): H. 71 cm, Diam. 44 cm
Candlesticks (2): H. 75 cm, Diam. 34 cm
The Confucius Museum in Qufu, Shandong Province

Inscription: 雍正年制 (*Yongzheng nianzhi*)

All the Qing emperors had great respect for Confucius and recognized his special significance in China's history. During his reign, the Yongzheng emperor visited the Temple of Confucius. This magnificent set of five painted-enamel altar vessels was his gift to the Kong family. Enamel is a colored coating applied on a solid body such as metalware.

The five-piece altar set includes an incense burner with a short neck under the mouth, a round belly, and a pair of long and curved, standing handles. At the bottom of the round belly are three hooved legs. The copper body of the vessel is coated with polychrome enamel in a design of peony and lotus scrolls. At the bottom, a vertical inscription in blue regular script translates as "Made in the Yongzheng reign."

There are a pair of vases, each with a trumpet mouth and a pair of dragon-shaped handles. Constructed in copper, the vases are relatively tall; each has a globular belly and a splayed ring foot. They are decorated with peony and lotus scrolls. Six raised gilt rings that wrap horizontally around the vase are distributed from top to bottom. On the foot rim is a red inscription that translates as "Made in the Yongzheng reign."

The set includes a pair of double-tiered candlestands composed of a round column, receptacle dishes, and a splayed foot. A candleprick is placed on the top dish. The stand is made of copper, and the body is decorated with peony and lotus scrolls. On the foot rim is a red inscription that translates as "Made in the Yongzheng reign."

LWS

37

Covered incense burner with crane feet

清代 景泰蓝三鹤足鼎

Qing dynasty (1644–1911)

Cloisonné enamel and gilt copper

H. 63 cm, W. 34.5 cm

The Confucius Museum in Qufu, Shandong Province

Intricately patterned with filigree filled with richly colored enamel, this type of unique metalware reached a high level of sophistication during the Jingtai reign of the Ming dynasty. Due to their usual blue ground or dominant color, these highly decorative objects came to be called *Jingtailan* (blue ware of the Jingtai reign). The English term for *Jingtailan* is cloisonné enamel.

This cloisonné vessel has a flat lip, a straight-sided mouth, and a contracted neck on a broad shoulder. Two dragon handles are attached to the shoulders and three cranes serve as its legs. The neck is decorated with a thundercloud scroll-meander pattern, the shoulder with a lily-petal motif, and the flattened belly with a deer motif among scrolling flowers and tendrils. The vessel's copper lid is decorated with a flower-and-bird design in openwork.

LWS

38
Beaded court necklace
清代　朝珠
Qing dynasty (1644–1911)
Gemstones and coral
L. (circumference) 98 cm
The Confucius Museum in Qufu, Shandong Province

Beaded court necklaces evolved from Buddhist rosaries. In general, a beaded court necklace consists of the following six parts: regular beads, four *fotou* (Buddha head) spacer beads, a corded precious stone for the back, three strings of counting beads, the main pendant, and three smaller pendants. This court necklace has 108 coral beads punctuated by four jadeite *fotou* beads at the interval of every 27 coral beads, a turquoise-colored cord for the jadeite back stone, an amethyst main pendant, and three strings of counting beads in jadeite. Each of the

strings has ten counting beads but is separately finished with a small ruby, emerald, or amethyst pendant. The materials used for beaded court necklaces are rare and precious. They usually have a plain finish to show off their natural beauty and textures. As a symbol of status, such necklaces were limited to the particular ranks and groups of people specified in the *Collected Statutes of the Great Qing (Da Qing huidian)*: "Those who are qualified to wear imperial beaded court necklaces are princes and dukes; civil officials of the fifth rank and above; military officers of the fourth rank and above; members of the imperial academy and divination masters; ministers and provincial chiefs; imperial body guards; princesses, wives of princes and dukes; and any female with the appointed title of virtuous woman of the fifth rank and above. Officials below the fifth rank are not allowed to wear beaded court necklaces."

LWS

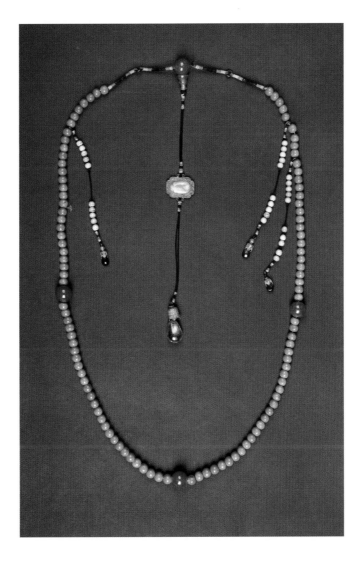

Bibliography

Agnew, Christopher S. "Culture and Power in the Making of the Descendents [sic] of Confucius, 1300–1800." PhD diss., Univ. of Washington, 2006.

———. "Memory and Power in Qufu: Inscribing the Past of Confucius' Descendants," *Journal of Family History* 34, no. 4 (2009): 327–43 DOI:10.1177/ 0363199009337393.

An, Hwi-jun 安辉浚. *Chosŏn wangjo sillok ŭi sŏhwa saryo* 朝鲜王朝实录의书画史料 [Historical materials on calligraphy and painting from the *Veritable Records of the Choson dynasty*]. Kyŏnggi-do Sŏngnam-si: Hanguk Chŏngsin Munhwa Yŏnguwŏn, 1983.

An Mengsong 安梦松. *Kongsheng quanshu* 孔圣全书 [Complete writings of the sage Confucius]. Nanjing: Zongwen shushe, 1599.

Baba Harukichi (or Haruyoshi) 马场春吉. *Kō Mō seiseki zukan* 孔孟圣迹图鉴 [Reflections in pictures of the traces of the sages Confucius and Mencius]. Tokyo: Santō bunka kenkyūkai, 1940.

———. *Kōshi seiseki shi* 孔子圣迹志 [Treatise on the traces of the sage Confucius]. Tokyo: Daitō bunka kyōkai, 1934.

Ban Gu 班固. *Hanshu* 汉书 [History of the Former Han]. Beijing Univ. punctuated and annotated edition. Beijing: Zhonghua shuju, 1962.

Beijing tushuguan cang huaxiang taben huibian 北京图书馆藏画像拓本汇编 [Pictorial rubbings in the Beijing Library]. Vol. 1. Compiled by Beijing tushuguan shanben bu jinshi zu. Beijing: Shumu wenxian chubanshe, 1993.

Beijing tushuguan guji zhenben congkan 北京图书馆古籍珍本丛刊 [Collectanea of rare books in the Beijing Library]. Vol. 23. Beijing: Shumu wenxian chubanshe, 1988.

Belsky, Richard. *Localities at the Center: Native Place, Space, and Power in Late Imperial Beijing*. Cambridge, Mass.: Harvard Univ. Asia Center, 2005.

Billioud, Sébastien and Joël Thoraval. "*Jiaohua*: The Confucian Revival in China as an Educative Project." Translated by Nina Lewin Jalladeau. *China Perspectives*, 2007, no. 4:4–20.

Brashier, Kenneth E. "Wantonly distorting the past." Ken Brashier's website, http://people.reed.edu/ ~brashiek/syllabi/Poster/index.html (accessed October 1, 2009).

Brinker, Helmut. "Ch'an Portraits in a Landscape." *Archives of Asian Art* 27 (1973–74): 8–29.

Chavannes, Édouard. *Mission archéologique dans la Chine septentrionale* [Archaeological mission in North China]. Vol. 6. Paris: Leroux, 1909.

Chen, Hsi-yuan. "Confucianism Encounters Religion: The Formation of Religious Discourse and the Confucian Movement in Modern China." PhD diss., Harvard Univ., 1999.

Chen Lü 陈旅. *Anyatang ji* 安雅堂集 [Collected writings of Chen Lü]. In *Yingyin Wenyuange Siku quanshu* 影印文渊阁四库全书 [Facsimile reproduction of the Wenyuange Hall Comprehensive books of the Four Treasuries], vol. 1213. Reprint, Taipei: Taiwan shangwu yinshuguan, 1983.

Chen Shou 陈寿. *Sanguo zhi Weishu* 三国志魏书 [Record of the Three Kingdoms: History of the Wei]. Beijing: Zhonghua shuju, 1962.

Chibi fu shuhua tezhan 赤壁赋书画特展 [Special exhibition of calligraphy and paintings of the Rhapsody on the Red Cliff]. Compiled by Guoli gugong bowuyuan 国立故宫博物院. Taipei: Guoli gugong bowuyuan, 1984.

Clunas, Craig. *Empire of Great Brightness: Visual and Material Cultures of Ming China, 1368–1644*. Honolulu: Univ. of Hawaii Press, 2007.

Csikszentmihalyi, Mark. "Confucius." In *The Rivers of Paradise: Moses, Buddha, Confucius, Jesus, and Muhammad as Religious Founders*, edited by David Noel Freedman and Michael J. McClymond, pp. 233–308. Grand Rapids, Mich.: W. B. Eerdsman, 2001.

———. "Confucius and the *Analects* in the Han." In *Confucius and the Analects*, edited by Brian van Norden, pp. 134–62. Oxford: Oxford Univ. Press, 2002.

Confucius: À l'aube de l'humanisme chinois. Paris: Réunion des musées nationaux; Barcelona: Fundacio la Caixa, 2003. Published in conjunction with the exhibition at the Musée National des Arts Asiatiques-Guimet.

Da zai Kongzi 大哉孔子 [Great is Confucius]. Compiled by Zhang Zuoyao 张作耀. Hong Kong: Heping tushu youxian gongsi, 1991.

Demattè, Paola. "Christ and Confucius: Accommodating Christian and Chinese Beliefs." In *China on Paper: European and Chinese Works from the Late Sixteenth to the Early Nineteenth Century*, edited by Marcia Reed and Paola Demattè, pp. 29–51. Los Angeles: Getty Research Institute, 2007.

Dickinson, Gary and Linda Wrigglesworth. *Imperial Wardrobe*. Berkeley: Ten Speed Press, 2000.

Dictionary of Ming Biography, 1368–1644. Edited by L. Carrington Goodrich and Chaoying Fang. New York: Columbia Univ. Press, 1976.

Eminent Chinese of the Ch'ing Period (1644–1912). Edited by Arthur W. Hummel, Jr. Reprint, Taipei: Ch'engwen Publishing Co., 1967.

Encyclopedia of Confucianism. Edited by Xinzhong Yao. London: RoutledgeCurzon, 2003.

Erickson, Susan. "*Que* Pillars at the Wu Family Cemetery and Related Structures in Shandong Province." In *Rethinking Recarving*, pp. 111–31.

Fan Ye 范晔. *Hou Hanshu* 后汉书 [History of the Later Han]. Beijing: Zhonghua shuju, 1965.

Farmer, J. Michael. "Art, Education, and Power: Illustrations in the Stone Chamber of Wen Weng." *T'oung Pao* 86 (2000): 100–35.

Foulk, T. Griffith and Robert H. Sharf. "On the Ritual Use of Ch'an Portraiture in Medieval China." *Cahiers d'Extrême-Asie* 7 (1993–94): 149–219.

Gardner, Daniel K. *The Four Books: The Teachings of the Later Confucian Tradition*. Indianapolis: Hackett Publishing. 2007.

Garrett, Valerie. *Chinese Dress: From the Qing Dynasty to the Present*. Tokyo & Rutland, Vt.: Tuttle Publishing, 2007.

Gu Chuanxiang 谷传祥. *Qufu lüyou daguan* 曲阜旅游大观 [Overview of touring in Qufu]. Ji'nan: Shandong huabao chubanshe, 1999.

Gujin tushu jicheng 古今图书集成 [Collected illustrations and texts, ancient and modern]. Compiled by Jiang Tingxi 蒋廷锡 et al. 1726. Reprint, Shanghai: Zhonghua shuju, 1934.

Huainanzi 淮南子 [Masters of Huainan]. Compiled by Liu An 刘安. Shanghai: Shangwu yinshuguan, 1919.

Huang Jinxing [Chin-hsing] 黄进兴. "Kongmiao de jiegou yu chongzu" 孔庙的结构于重组 [The structure of the Confucius Temple in reorganization]. *Dangdai* 当代 [Contemporary] 86 (June 1, 1993): 120–33.

Huayang xian zhi 华阳县志 [Gazetteer of Huayang county]. Compiled by Fan Xuepu 樊学圃and Zeng Jian 曾鉴. 1934. Vol. 3 of *Zhongguo difangzhi jicheng: Sichuan fuxian zhi ji* 中国地方志集成. 四川府县志辑 [Compendium of Chinese local gazetteers: A collection of prefectural and county gazetteers of Sichuan]. Reprint, Chengdu: Ba Shu shushe, 1992.

An Illustrated Life of Confucius: From Tablets in the Temple at Chufu Shantung. Reprint of Kong Xianlan's 1874 edition with English translations interspersed. Translated by H. P. Lair and L. C. Wang. 1910. Reprint, Taipei: Ch'eng Wen Publishing Co., 1972.

In Search of the Supernatural: The Written Record. Translated by Kenneth DeWoskin and J. I. Crump, Jr. Stanford: Stanford Univ. Press, 1996.

Jang, Scarlett. "The Eunuch Agency Directorate of Ceremonial and the Ming Imperial Publishing Enterprise." In *Culture, Courtiers, and Competition: The Ming Court (1368–1644)*, edited by David M. Robinson, pp. 116–85. Cambridge, Mass.: Harvard Univ. Asia Center, 2008.

Jensen, Lionel M. *Manufacturing Confucianism: Chinese Traditions and Universal Civilization*. Durham, N.C.: Duke Univ. Press, 1997.

Jing, Jun. *The Temple of Memories: History, Power, and Morality in a Chinese Village*. Stanford: Stanford Univ. Press, 1996.

Kaji Nobuyuki 加地伸行. *Kōshi gaden: Seiseki zu ni miru Koshi rurō no shogai to oshie* 孔子 画伝: 聖蹟図 に み る 孔 子流 浪 の 生涯 と 教 [Pictorial biography of Confucius: Confucius's life of wandering and doctrine as seen in the pictures of the sage's traces]. Tokyo: Shūeisha, 1991.

Kinney, Anne Behnke. *Representations of Childhood and Youth in Early China*. Stanford: Stanford Univ. Press, 2004.

Knoblock, John. "The History of the *Xunzi* Text." http://www.as.miami.edu/phi/bio/Buddha/xunwork.htm (accessed August 2, 2009)

Kong Chuan 孔传. *Dongjia zaji* 东家杂记 [Miscellaneous records of the Eastern House]. 1134. Reprinted in *Kongzi wenhua daquan* 孔子文化大全 [Comprehensive collection of Confucian civilization]. Ji'nan: Shandong youyi shushe, 1990.

Kong Demao 孔德懋. "Kongfu neizhai yishi" 孔府内宅轶事 [Anecdotes from the inner household of the Kong establishment]. 1982. Reprinted in *Tianxia diyi jia*, pp. 147–216. Beijing: Xinhua chubanshe, 1995.

Kong Jifen 孔继汾. *Kongshi jia yi* 孔氏家儀 [Kong family ritual]. Reprint. Beijing: Beijing chubanshe, 2005.

———. *Queli wenxian kao* 阙里文献考 [Research on documents in Queli]. Qufu, 1762. Reprint, Taipei: Zhongguo wenxian chubanshe, 1966.

Kong Yuancuo 孔元措. *Kongshi zuting guangji* 孔氏祖庭广记 [An expanded record of the Kong lineage]. 1242. Reprinted in *Baibu congshu jicheng* 百部丛书集成 [One hundred collected collectanea], vol. 65, no. 1. Taipei: Yiwen yinshuguan, 1967.

Kong Zhaoxi 孔昭玺. *Zengbu Kongting zhaiyao* 增补孔庭摘要 [Essentials concerning the Kong family, expanded]. Qufu, 1897. Reprinted in *Kongzi wenhua daquan* 孔子文化大全 [Comprehensive collection of Confucian civilization]. Ji'nan: Shandong youyi shushe, 1990.

Kongzi 孔子 [Confucius]. *Hao ertong lizhi congshu* 好儿童励志丛书 [Collected books for good children pursuing their goals], vol. 14. Taipei: Shiyi wenhua shiye gufen youxian gongsi, 2003. Comic book for ages 7+, see http://www.asianparent.com/index.asp?PageAction=VIEWPROD&ProdID=290 (accessed August 7, 2009).

Kongzi jiayu 孔子家语 [Sayings of the Confucians]. Annotated by Wang Su 王肃. Taipei: Shijie shuju, 1962.

Kongzi: Jinian Kongzi danchen 2540 zhounian 孔子: 纪念孔子诞辰2540周年 [Confucius: Commemorating the 2540th anniversary of Confucius's birth]. Compiled by Shoudu bowuguan 首都博物馆. Beijing: Zhongguo jiaoyu tushu jinchukou gongsi, 1989.

Kongzi shengji tu 孔子圣迹图 [Pictures of the traces of the sage Confucius]. Compiled by Li Bingwei 李炳卫. Beijing: Beiping minshe, 1934. Facsimile reprints, Taipei: Wensi chubanshe, 1984; Shijiazhuang: Hebei meishu chubanshe, 1996.

Kongzi shengji tu 孔子圣迹图 [Pictures of the traces of the sage Confucius]. In *Zhongguo hua guben xinshang congshu* 中国画孤本欣赏丛书 [Collected works on the appreciation of unique versions of Chinese paintings], Tianjin: Yangliuqing huashe, 1996.

Kongzi shengji tu 孔子圣迹图 / *Illustration of Major Events in Confucius' Life* [sic]. Edited by Kong Xianglin 孔祥林. In *Kongzi wenhua daquan* 孔子文化大全 [Comprehensive collection of Confucian civilization], ed. Miao Fenglin 苗枫林. Ji'nan: Shandong meishu chubanshe, 1988.

Kongzi shengji tu 孔子圣迹图 / *The Sage's Traces Pictures of Confucius* [sic]. Edited by Liu Yang 刘映. Beijing: Xianzhuang shuju, 2005.

Kongzi shijia pu 孔子世家谱 [Genealogy of Confucius's hereditary house]. Compiled by Kong Decheng 孔德成. Qufu, 1937. Reprinted in Kongzi wenhua daquan 孔子文化大全 [Comprehensive collection of Confucian civilization]. Ji'nan: Shandong youyi shushe, 1990.

Kongzi xiang, Yanshenggong ji furen xiaoxiang 孔子像, 衍圣公及夫人肖像 / *Portraits of Confucius, Portraits of the Dukes of Yansheng and Their Wives* [sic]. Compiled by Shandong sheng Qufu shi wenwu guanli weiyuanhui 山东省曲阜市文物管理委员会. Ji'nan: Shandong youyi shushe, 1987.

Kongzi xingjiao tu 孔子行教图 / *Confucius Journeys Through Pictures* [sic]. Taipei: Zuanshi chubanshe, 1974.

Kōshi no furusato yonsennen ten: Santō-shō bunbutsu 孔子の原郷 (ふるさと) 四千年展: 山東省文物 [Exhibition of 4000 years of the hometown of Confucius: Cultural relics from Shandong]. Compiled by Kodai Oriento Hakubutsukan 古代オリエント博物館. Tokyo: Asahi Tsūshinsha, 1992.

Kramers, Robert P. *K'ung Tzŭ Chia Yü: The School Sayings of Confucius*. Leiden: E. J. Brill, 1950.

Lamberton, Abigail. "The Kongs of Qufu: Power and Privilege in Late Imperial China." In Wilson, *On Sacred Grounds*, pp. 297–332.

Laufer, Berthold. "Confucius and His Portraits." *The Open Court* 26 (1912): 147–68 and 202–18.

Legge, James. *The She King*. Vol. 4 of *The Chinese Classics*. Reprint, Taipei: Southern Materials Center, 1985.

Li Daoyuan 郦道元. *Shuijing zhu jiao* 水经注校 [Collated annotations to the *Rivers Classics*]. Collated by Wang Guowei 王国维. Shanghai: Renmin chubanshe, 1984.

Li Jingming 李景明. *Jiazu shixi* 家族世系 [Family lineage]. Vol. 2 of *Kongzi jiazu quanshu* 孔子家族全书 [Complete books of Confucius's lineage]. Shenyang: Liaohai chubanshe, 2000.

Li Jinshan 李锦山. *Lunan Han huaxiang shi yanjiu* 鲁南汉画像石研究 [Research on Han pictorial stones from Southern Lu]. Beijing: Zhishi chanquan chubanshe, 2008.

Liu, Cary A. et al. *Recarving China's Past: Art, Archaeology, and Architecture of the "Wu Family Shrines."* New Haven & London: Yale Univ. Press, 2005.

Lü Weiqi 吕维祺. *Shengxian xiangzan* 圣贤像赞 [Portraits and encomia for the sage and worthies]. 1632. Reprinted in *Kongzi wenhua daquan* 孔子文化大全 [Comprehensive collection of Confucian civilization]. Ji'nan: Shandong youyi shushe 1989.

Luo Chenglie 骆承烈. *Huaxiang zhong de Kongzi* 画像中的孔子 / *The Figures of Confucius* (sic). Shanghai: Guji chubanshe, 2003.

MacFarquhar, Roderick and Michael Schoenhals. *Mao's Last Revolution*. Cambridge, Mass.: Belknap Press of Harvard Univ. Press, 2006.

Makeham, John. *Lost Soul: "Confucianism" in Contemporary Chinese Academic Discourse*. Harvard-Yenching Institute monograph series, vol. 64. Cambridge, Mass.: Harvard Univ. Asia Center, 2008.

Min'guo Huayang xian zhi. 民国华阳县志 [Republic-era gazetteer of Huayang county]. See *Huayang xian zhi*.

Min'guo Quxian zhi 民国衢县志 [Republic-era Gazetteer of Quzhou county]. See *Quxian zhi*.

Mingshi 明史 [History of the Ming]. Compiled by Zhang Tingyu 张廷玉 et al. 1739. Punctuated and annotated edition. Beijing: Zhonghua shuju, 1974.

Murray, Julia K. "The Global Rebranding of Confucius." In *China in 2008: A Year of Great Significance*, edited by Jeffrey Wasserstrom, Kate Merkel-Hess, and Kenneth Pomeranz, pp. 263–70. Lanham, Md.: Rowman & Littlefield, 2009.

———. "The Hangzhou *Portraits of Confucius and Seventy-two Disciples* (*Sheng xian tu*): Art in the Service of Politics." *Art Bulletin* 74, no. 1 (March 1992): 7–18.

———. "'Idols' in the Temple: Icons and the Cult of Confucius." *The Journal of Asian Studies* 68, no. 2 (May 2009): 371–411.

———. "Illustrations of the Life of Confucius: Their Evolution, Functions, and Significance in Late Ming China." *Artibus Asiae* 57, no. 1–2 (1997): 73–134.

———. *Mirror of Morality: Chinese Narrative Illustration and Confucian Ideology*. Honolulu: Univ. of Hawaii Press, 2007.

———. "Pedagogue on the Go: Portraits of Confucius as an Itinerant Teacher." In *Bridges to Heaven: Essays in Honor of Professor Wen C. Fong*, edited by Jerome Silbergeld, Dora C. Y. Ching, Alfreda Murck, and Judith Smith. Princeton: Tang Center for East Asian Art (forthcoming).

———. "Portraits of Confucius: Icons and Iconoclasm." *Oriental Art* 47, no. 3 (2001): 17–28.

———. "The Temple of Confucius and Pictorial Biographies of the Sage." *The Journal of Asian Studies* 55, no. 2 (May 1996): 269–300.

———. "Varied Views of the Sage: Illustrated Narratives of the Life of Confucius." In Wilson, *On Sacred Grounds*, pp. 222–64.

Nylan, Michael. *The Five "Confucian" Classics*. New Haven: Yale Univ. Press, 2001.

Nylan, Michael and Thomas A Wilson. *The Lives of Confucius: Civilization's Greatest Sage Through the Ages*. New York: Random House, Doubleday Religion, 2010.

Pipan Qufu "San Kong" 批判曲阜"三孔" [Criticize Qufu's "Three Kong"]. Compiled by Shandongsheng bowuguan and Qufu xian wenwu guanli weiyuanhui 山东省博物馆; 曲阜县文物管理委员会. Beijing: Wenwu chubanshe, 1974.

Plaks, Andrew H. *Ta Hsüeh and Chung Yung*. London & New York: Penguin, 2003.

Powers, Martin J. *Art and Political Expression in Early China*. New Haven & London: Yale Univ. Press, 1991.

———. "Pictorial Art and Its Public in Early Imperial China." *Art History* 7, no. 2 (June 1984): 135–63.

Qianlong Qufu xian zhi 乾隆曲阜县志. See *Qufu xian zhi*.

Qing huajia shishi 清画家诗史 [History of Qing painters' poetry]. Compiled by Li Junzhi 李浚之. 1930. In *Qingdai zhuanji congkan, yilin lei* 清代传记丛刊. 艺林类 [Biographical collections of the Qing period: The world of art]. Reprint, Taipei: Mingwen shuju, 1985.

Qingshi gao 清史稿. See *Xinjiao ben Qingshi gao*.

Qiu Jiaxing 邱家兴. "Shouguang shengren mu de chuanshuo yu shishi" 寿光圣人母的传说与史实 [Legends and facts about Shouguang's sage mother]. *Shouguang ribao* 寿光日报 [Shouguang daily], April 18, 2009. Posted on "Zhenguan Li shi yanjiu" 斟灌李氏研究 [Research on the Li clan of Zhenguan], in Li Bosheng 李博生, Zhenguan chunqiu 斟灌春秋 [Chronicles of Zhenguan]. http://zgcqls.com/research/3-10.htm (accessed August 11, 2009).

Queli guangzhi 阙里广誌. [Broadened gazetteer of Queli]. Compiled by Song Ji 宋际 and Song Qingchang 宋庆长, 1673. Reprinted Qufu: Kong Runzhou, 1870.

Queli zhi 阙里志 [Gazetteer of Queli]. Compiled by Chen Gao 陈镐, 1505. First expanded edition compiled by Kong Honggan 孔弘干, 1552. Reprinted in *Beijing tushuguan guji zhenben congkan*, vol. 23, pp. 393–897. A second expanded edition, completed in 1599 and printed in 1609, was compiled by Kong Zhencong 孔贞丛. A third expanded edition compiled by Kong Yinzhi 孔胤植 in the 17th c., has been reprinted in Siku quanshu cunmu congshu, ser. 2, vol. 76.

Qufu Kongmiao jianzhu 曲阜孔庙建筑 [The architecture of the Confucius Temple in Qufu]. Compiled by Nanjing Gongxueyuan jianzhuxi 南京工学院建筑系 and Qufu wenwu guanli weiyuanhui 曲阜管理委员会. Beijing: Zhongguo jianzhu gongye chubanshe, 1987.

Qufu Kongmiao, Konglin, Kongfu 曲阜孔庙·孔林·孔府 [Qufu's Confucius Temple, Cemetery, and Mansion]. Compiled by Chen Chuanping 陈传平. In *Zhongguo shijie yichan congshu* 中国世界遗产丛书 [World heritage sites in China series]. Xi'an: San Qin chubanshe, 2004.

Qufu: Kongzi de guxiang 曲阜: 孔子的故乡 / *Qufu, The Native Place of Confucius*. Compiled by Shandongsheng Qufushi Wenwu guanli weiyuanhui 山东省曲阜市文物管理委员会. Beijing: Wenwu chubanshe, 1990.

Qufu xian zhi 曲阜县志 [Gazetteer of Qufu county]. Compiled by Pan Xiang 潘相 et al. 1774. Reprinted in *Xinxiu fangzhi congkan* 新修方志丛刊 [Collection of revised local gazetteers], no. 85; *Shandong fangzhi* 山东方志 [Shandong gazetteers], no. 5. Taipei: Taiwan xuesheng shuju, 1968.

Quxian zhi 衢县志 [Gazetteer of Quzhou county]. Compiled by Zheng Yongxi 郑永禧. 1926. Reprinted in *Zhongguo difangzhi jicheng: Zhejiang fuxian zhiji* 中国地方志集成, 浙江府县志辑 [Compendium of Chinese local gazetteers: A collection of prefecture and county gazetteers of Zhejiang], vol. 55. Shanghai: Shanghai shudian, 1993.

Rethinking Recarving: Ideals, Practices, and Problems of the "Wu Family Shrines" and Han China. Edited by Naomi Noble Richard. Princeton: Princeton Univ. Art Museum; New Haven & London: Yale Univ. Press, 2008.

RoutledgeCurzon Encyclopedia of Confucianism. See *Encyclopedia of Confucianism.*

Scripta Sinica (Zhongyang yanjiu yuan Hanji dianzi wenxian 中央研究院汉籍电子文献). Online database of the Taipei Academia Sinica. http://dbo.sinica.edu.tw/~tdbproj/handy1/.

Selected Poems of Su Tung-p'o. Translated by Burton Watson. Port Townsend, Wash.: Copper Canyon Press, 1994.

Shandong sheng bowuguan 山东省博物馆. "Fajue Ming Zhu Tan mu jishi" 发掘明朱檀墓纪实 [Report on the excavation of the Ming tomb of Zhu Tan]. *Wenwu* 文物, 1972, no. 5:25–36.

Shengji zhi tu 圣迹之图 / *The Pictures About Confucius' Life* (sic). Compiled by Shandongsheng Qufushi wenwu guanli weiyuanhui 山东省曲阜市文物管理委员会. In *Kongzi wenhua daquan* 孔子文化大全 [Comprehensive collection of Confucian civilization]. Ji'nan: Shandong General Press, 1988.

Shi Ke 石可. *Kongzi shiji tu, Lunyu zhenyan yin* 孔子事迹图．论语箴言印 [Pictures of the deeds of Confucius; Seals with maxims from the *Analects*]. Ji'nan: Qi Lu shushe, 1987.

Siggstedt, Mette. "Forms of Fate: An Investigation of the Relationship between Formal Portraiture, Especially Ancestral Portraits, and Physiognomy (*xiangshu*) in China." In *International Colloquium on Chinese Art History* (1991), part 2, pp. 717–48. Taipei: National Palace Museum, 1991.

Siku quanshu cunmu congshu. Shi bu, Zhuanji lei 四库全书存目丛书．史部，传记类 [Collectanea of titles preserved in the *Complete books of the Four Treasuries*, History section, Biography classification], ser. 2, vol. 76. Ji'nan: Qi Lu shushe chubanshe, 1997.

Sima Qian 司马迁. *Shiji* 史记 [Historical records]. Beijing Univ. punctuated and annotated edition. Beijing: Zhonghua shuju, 1982.

———. *Selections from Records of the Historian.* Translated by Hsienyi and Gladys Yang. Beijing: Foreign Languages Press, 1979.

Sommer, Deborah A. "Destroying Confucius: Iconoclasm in the Confucian Temple." In Wilson, *On Sacred Grounds*, pp. 95–133.

———. "Images into Words: Ming Confucian Iconoclasm." *National Palace Museum Bulletin* 29 (1994):1–24.

Soushen ji 搜神记 [Record of searching for the supernatural]. Compiled by Gan Bao 干宝. Reprint, Taipei, Shijie shuju, 1962.

Soymié, Michel. "L'entrevue de Confucius et de Hiang T'o." *Journal Asiatique* 242 (1954): 311–92.

Spiro, Audrey. *Contemplating the Ancients: Aesthetic and Social Issues in Early Chinese Portraiture.* Berkeley & Los Angeles: Univ. of California Press, 1990.

Stuart, Jan and Evelyn S. Rawski. *Worshiping the Ancestors: Chinese Commemorative Portraits.* Washington D.C. and Stanford: Smithsonian Institution and Stanford Univ. Press, 2001.

Su Shi. See *Selected poems of Su Tung-p'o.*

Temple and Cemetery of Confucius and the Kong Family Mansion in Qufu / Qufu Kongmiao Konglin Kongfu 曲阜孔庙孔林孔府. Compiled by Kong Deping 孔德平 et al. English translation by Liu Haixia 刘海霞. Beijing: New World Press, 2007.

Tianxia diyi jia 天下第一家 [First family under heaven]. Compiled by Wang Yongji 汪永基 and Kong Xiangmin 孔祥民. Beijing: Xinhua chubanshe, 1995.

Tillman, Hoyt Cleveland. "Zhu Xi's Prayers to the Spirit of Confucius and Claim to the Transmission of the Way." *Philosophy East and West* 54, no. 4 (Oct. 2004): 489–513.

Tsai Chih Chung. *Confucius Speaks: Words to Live By.* Translated by Brian Bruya. New York: Anchor Books, 1996.

Tsang, Kabo. "In Her Majesty's Service: Women Painters in China at the Court of the Empress Dowager Cixi." In *Local/Global: Women Artists in the Nineteenth Century.* Edited by Deborah Cherry and Janice Helland, pp. 35–57. Aldershot, UK: Ashgate Press, 2006.

Walton, Linda A. *Academies and Society in Southern Sung China.* Honolulu: Univ. of Hawaii Press, 1999.

Wang Jia 王嘉. *Shiyi ji* 拾遗记 [Recorded gleanings]. Reprinted in *Baibu congshu jicheng* 百部丛书集成 [One hundred collected collectanea], ser. 9. Taipei: Yiwen yinshuguan, 1966.

Wang Liang. "The Confucian Temple Tragedy of the Cultural Revolution." Translated by Curtis Dean Smith. In Wilson, *On Sacred Grounds*, pp. 376–96.

Wang Liang. See also Yazi.

Wang Qi 王圻. *Sancai tuhui* 三才图会 [Pictorial compendium of the three powers]. 1607. Reprint, Taipei: Chengwen chubanshe, 1970.

Wang Shucun 王树村. *Kongzi baitu* 孔子百图 [One hundred pictures of Confucius]. Guangzhou: Lingnan meishu chubanshe, 1997.

Weidner [Haufler], Marsha et al. *Views from Jade Terrace: Chinese Women Artists 1300–1912*. Indianapolis & New York: Indianapolis Museum of Art & Rizzolli, 1988.

Wilson, Thomas A. *Confucian Gods and the Rites to Venerate Them* (unpublished manuscript).

———. "Introduction: Culture, Society, Politics, and the Cult of Confucius." In Wilson, *On Sacred Grounds*, pp. 1–40.

———, ed. *On Sacred Grounds: Culture, Society, Politics, and the Formation of the Temple of Confucius*. Cambridge, Mass.: Harvard Univ. Asia Center, 2002.

———. "The Ritual Formation of Confucian Orthodoxy and the Descendants of the Sage." *The Journal of Asian Studies* 55, no. 3 (Aug. 1996): 559–84.

———. "Ritualizing Confucius / Kongzi: The Family and State Cults of the Sage of Culture in Imperial China." In Wilson, *On Sacred Grounds*, pp. 43–94.

———. "Sacrifice and the Imperial Cult of Confucius." *History of Religions* 41 (2002): 251–87.

Wu Hung. "The Earliest Pictorial Representations of Ape Tales: An Interdisciplinary Study of Early Chinese Narrative Art." *T'oung Pao* ser. 2, vol. 73, nos. 1–3 (1987): 86–112.

Xichao xinyu 熙朝新语 [New sayings from the brilliant court]. Compiled by Xu Xilin 徐锡麟 and Qian Yong 钱泳. 1824. Reprinted in *Jindai Zhongguo shiliao congkan, sanbian, di si ji* 近代中国史料丛刊三编，第四辑 [Collection of historical materials on modern China, third series, fourth compilation], vol. 36. Yonghe city, Taipei county: Wenhai chubanshe, 1984.

Xin Qingshi, ben ji 新清史-本纪 [New Qing history: Basic annals]. In *Scripta Sinica*.

Xinjiao ben Qingshi gao 新校本清史稿 [Newly revised Draft history of Qing]. In *Scripta Sinica*.

Xinkan Shengji tu ji 新刊圣迹图记 [Record of the new publication of *Pictures of the Sage's Traces*]. Compiled by Kong Xianlan 孔宪兰. Qufu, 1874.

Yazi 亚子 [Wang Liang 王良]. *Kongfu da jienan* 孔府大劫难 [The great plundering of the Kong establishment]. Hong Kong: Tiandi tushu youxian gongsi, 1991.

Yu Jianhua 俞剑华. *Zhongguo meishujia renming cidian* 中国美术家人名辞典 [Dictionary of Chinese artist names]. Shanghai: Renmin meishu chubanshe, 1981.

Zhang Qiyun 张其昀, ed. *Kong Meng shengji tushuo* 孔孟圣迹图说 [Explanation of the pictures of the sages Confucius and Mencius]. Taipei: Zhonghua wenhua chuban shiye she, 1960.

Zhang Yanyuan 张彦远. *Lidai minghua ji* 历代名画记 [Record of famous paintings through the ages]. 847. Reprinted in *Huashi congshu* 画史丛书 [Compendium of painting histories], edited by Yu Anlan 于安澜. Shanghai: Renmin meishu chubanshe, 1963.

Zhang Yingji 张英基. "Kong Zhaoqian zaju 'Tangfu qiu si', 'Sanghua' shangxi" 孔昭虔杂剧《蕩婦秋思》、《葬花》赏析 [An appreciation of Kong Zhaoqian's *zaju* dramas "Immoral Woman's Melancholy Thoughts of Autumn" and "Burying Flowers"]. http://blog.gmw.cn/u/73/archives/2005/8296.html [posted 2005/7/18 15:33:00] (accessed August 15, 2009).

Zhongguo gudai banhua congkan 中国古代版画丛刊 [Series on Chinese ancient printed pictures]. Shanghai: Gudian wenxue chubanshe, 1958.

Zhongguo gudai banhua congkan, erbian 中国古代版画丛刊，二编 [Series on Chinese ancient printed pictures, second compilation]. Shanghai: Shanghai guji chubanshe, 1994.

Zhongguo huaxiang shi quanji 中国画像石全集 [Complete collection of Chinese pictorial stones]. Ji'nan: Shandong meishu chubanshe, 2000.

Zhu Xi 朱熹. *Sishu zhangju jizhu* 四书章句集注 [Collected sentence annotations of the Four Books]. Beijing: Beijing tushuguan chubanshe, 2006.

Zhuangzi jishi 庄子集释 [Collected explanations of the *Zhuangzi*]. Compiled by Guo Qingfan 郭庆藩. Beijing: Zhonghua shuju, 1961.

Zuantu huzhu Xunzi 纂图互注荀子 [Illustrated and annotated *Xunzi*]. Facsimile reprint in *Zhongguo zixue mingzhu jicheng* 中国子学名著集成 [Compendium of famous writings of Chinese philosophers], vol. 24. Taipei: Zhongguo zixue mingzhu jicheng bianyin jijinhui, 1977.

China Institute Gallery Exhibitions: 1966–2009

1. SELECTIONS OF CHINESE ART FROM PRIVATE COLLECTIONS IN THE METROPOLITAN AREA
   November 15, 1966–February 15, 1967
   Curator: Mrs. Gilbert Katz

2. ART STYLES OF ANCIENT SHANG
   April 5–June 11, 1967
   Curator: Jean Young

3. ANIMALS AND BIRDS IN CHINESE ART
   October 25, 1967–January 28, 1968
   Curator: Fong Chow

4. GARDENS IN CHINESE ART
   March 21–May 26, 1968
   Curator: Wan-go H.C. Weng

5. CHINESE JADE THROUGH THE CENTURIES
   October 24, 1968–January 26, 1969
   Curator: Joan M. Hartman

6. FOREIGNERS IN ANCIENT CHINESE ART
   March 27–May 25, 1969
   Curator: Ezekiel Schloss

7. CHINESE PAINTED ENAMELS
   October 23, 1969–February 1, 1970
   Curator: J.A. Lloyd Hyde

8. ALBUM LEAVES FROM THE SUNG AND YUAN DYNASTIES
   March 26–May 30, 1970
   Curator: C.C. Wang

9. MING PORCELAINS: A RETROSPECTIVE
   October 29, 1970–January 31, 1971
   Curator: Suzanne G. Valenstein

10. CHINESE SILK TAPESTRY: K'O-SSU
    March 24–May 27, 1971
    Curator: Jean Mailey

11. EARLY CHINESE GOLD AND SILVER
    October 21, 1971–January 30, 1972
    Curator: Dr. Paul Singer

12. DRAGONS IN CHINESE ART
    March 23–May 28, 1972
    Curator: Hugo Munsterberg

13. WINTRY FORESTS, OLD TREES: SOME LANDSCAPE THEMES IN CHINESE PAINTING
    October 26, 1972–January 28, 1973
    Curator: Richard Barnhart

14. CERAMICS IN THE LIAO DYNASTY: NORTH AND SOUTH OF THE GREAT WALL
    March 15–May 28, 1973
    Curator: Yutaka Mino

15. CHINA TRADE PORCELAIN: A STUDY IN DOUBLE REFLECTIONS
    October 25, 1973–January 27, 1974
    Curator: Claire le Corbeiller

16. TANTRIC BUDDHIST ART
    March 14–May 24, 1974
    Curator: Eleanor Olson

17. FRIENDS OF WEN CHENG-MING: A VIEW FROM THE CRAWFORD COLLECTION
    October 24, 1974–January 26, 1975
    Curators: Marc F. Wilson and Kwan S. Wong

18. ANCIENT CHINESE JADES FROM THE BUFFALO MUSEUM OF SCIENCE
    April 3–June 15, 1975
    Curator: Joan M. Hartman

19. ART OF THE SIX DYNASTIES: CENTURIES OF CHANGE AND INNOVATION
    October 29, 1975–February 1, 1976
    Curator: Annette L. Juliano

20. CHINA'S INFLUENCE ON AMERICAN CULTURE IN THE 18TH AND 19TH CENTURIES
    April 8–June 13, 1976
    Curators: Henry Trubner and William Jay Rathburn
    (Exhibition traveled to the Seattle Art Museum, October 7–November 28, 1976.)

21. CHINESE FOLK ART IN AMERICAN COLLECTIONS: EARLY 15TH THROUGH 20TH CENTURIES
    October 27, 1976–January 30, 1977
    Curator: Tseng Yu-Ho Ecke

22. EARLY CHINESE MINIATURES
    March 16–May 29, 1977
    Curator: Dr. Paul Singer

23. I-HSING WARE
    October 28, 1977–January 29, 1978
    Curator: Terese Tse Bartholomew
    (Exhibition traveled to the Nelson Gallery of Art, Kansas City, February 19–May 21, 1978, and the Asian Art Museum of San Francisco, June 16–September 21, 1978.)

24. EMBROIDERY OF IMPERIAL CHINA
    March 17–May 28, 1978
    Curator: Jean Mailey

25. ORIGINS OF CHINESE CERAMICS
    October 25, 1978–January 28, 1979
    Curator: Clarence F. Shangraw

26. ART OF THE HAN
    March 14–May 27, 1979
    Curator: Ezekiel Schloss

27. TREASURES FROM THE METROPOLITAN MUSEUM OF ART
    October 25–November 25, 1979
    Curator: Clarence F. Shangraw

28. CHINESE ART FROM THE NEWARK MUSEUM
    March 19–May 25, 1980
    Curators: Valrae Reynolds and Yen Fen Pei

29. CHINESE PORCELAINS IN EUROPEAN MOUNTS
    October 22, 1980–January 25, 1981
    Curator: Sir Francis Watson

30. FREEDOM OF CLAY AND BRUSH THROUGH SEVEN CENTURIES IN NORTHERN CHINA: TZ'U-CHOU TYPE WARES 960-1600 A.D.
    March 16–May 24, 1981
    Curator: Yutaka Mino
    (Exhibition originated at Indianapolis Museum of Art.)

31. THE ART OF CHINESE KNOTTING
    July 29–September 21, 1981
    Curator: Hsia-Sheng Chen

32. MASTERPIECES OF SUNG AND YUAN DYNASTY CALLIGRAPHY FROM THE JOHN M. CRAWFORD JR. COLLECTION
    October 21, 1981–January 31, 1982
    Curator: Kwan S. Wong, assisted by Stephen Addiss
    (Exhibition traveled to the Spencer Museum, University of Kansas, March 14–April 18, 1982.)

33. THE COMMUNION OF SCHOLARS: CHINESE ART AT YALE
    March 20–May 30, 1982
    Curator: Mary Gardner Neill
    (Exhibition traveled to the Museum of Fine Arts, Houston, June 22–August 22, 1982, and the Yale Art Gallery, New Haven, October 5, 1982–April 17, 1983.)

34. CHINA FROM WITHIN
    November 4–December 12, 1982
    A Smithsonian Institution Travelling Services Exhibition, organized by the International Photography Society in cooperation with the China Exhibition Agency, Beijing, and the Chinese Embassy, Washington, DC

35. BAMBOO CARVING OF CHINA
    March 18–May 29, 1983
    Curators: Wang Shixiang and Wan-go H.C. Weng
    (Exhibition traveled to The Nelson-Atkins Museum of Art, Kansas City, July 24–September 11, 1983, and the Asian Art Museum of San Francisco, October 3, 1983–January 15, 1984.)

36. CHINESE CERAMICS OF THE TRANSITIONAL PERIOD: 1620-1683
    October 21, 1983–January 29, 1984
    Curator: Stephen Little
    (Exhibition traveled to the Kimbell Art Museum, Fort Worth, May 26–August 26, 1984.)

37. MASTERPIECES OF CHINESE EXPORT PORCELAIN AND RELATED DECORA-TIVE ARTS FROM THE MOTTAHEDEH COLLECTION
February 10–March 7, 1984
U.S.-China 200 Bicentennial Exhibition, organized by Anita Christy

38. CHINESE TRADITIONAL ARCHITECTURE
April 6–June 10, 1984
Curator: Nancy Shatzman Steinhardt
(A permanent traveling exhibition of China Institute. Shown at Allegheny College, Meade-ville, PA, March 28–April 19, 1985; Marlboro College, Marlboro, VT, September 11–October 31, 1985; State University of New York, Binghamton, January 7–Febru-ary 27, 1986.)

39. CHINESE RARE BOOKS IN AMERICAN COLLECTIONS
October 20, 1984–January 29, 1985
Curator: Soren Edgren

40. THE SUMPTUOUS BASKET: CHINESE LACQUER WITH BASKETRY PANELS
March 20–June 3, 1985
Curator: James C.Y. Watt

41. KERNELS OF ENERGY, BONES OF EARTH: THE ROCK IN CHINESE ART
October 26, 1985–January 26, 1986
Curator: John Hay

42. PUPPETRY OF CHINA
April 19–June 29, 1986
Curator: Roberta Helmer Stalberg
Organized by the Center for Puppetry Arts, Atlanta

43. SELECTIONS OF CHINESE ART FROM PRIVATE COLLECTIONS
October 18, 1986–January 4, 1987
Exhibition celebrating the 60th Anniversary of China Institute and the 20th Anniversary of China Institute Gallery, organized by James C.Y. Watt and Annette L. Juliano.

44. 1987 NEW YEAR EXHIBITION

45. CHINESE FOLK ART
April 4–May 30, 1987
Curator: Nancy Zeng Berliner

46. RICHLY WOVEN TRADITIONS: COS-TUMES OF THE MIAO OF SOUTHWEST CHINA AND BEYOND
October 22, 1987–January 4, 1988
Curator: Theresa Reilly

47. 1988 NEW YEAR EXHIBITION
February 4–February 24, 1988

48. RITUAL AND POWER:
JADES OF ANCIENT CHINA
April 23–June 19, 1988
Curator: Elizabeth Childs-Johnson

49. STORIES FROM CHINA'S PAST
September 17–November 12, 1988
Organized by The Chinese Culture Center of San Francisco

50. 1989 NEW YEAR EXHIBITION: LANTERNS
January 28–February 25, 1989

51. MIND LANDSCAPES:
THE PAINTINGS OF C.C. WANG
April 3–May 27, 1989
Curator: Jerome Silbergeld

52. CHINA BETWEEN REVOLUTIONS: PHO-TOGRAPHY BY SIDNEY D. GAMBLE, 1917–1927
June 29–September 9, 1989
Organized by The Sidney D. Gamble Foundation for China Studies and China Institute in America

53. VIEWS FROM JADE TERRACE: CHINESE WOMEN ARTISTS, 1300–1912
October 5–December 2, 1989
Organized by Indianapolis Museum of Art

54. 1990 NEW YEAR EXHIBITION:
THE CHINESE EARTH–VIEWS OF NATURE
January–March 1990
Curator: Anita Christy

55. CLEAR AS CRYSTAL, RED AS FLAME: LATER CHINESE GLASS
April 21–June 16, 1990
Curator: Claudia Brown and Donald Robiner

56. THE ECCENTRIC PAINTERS OF YANGZHOU
October 20 December 15, 1990
Curator: Vito Giacalone

57. 1991 NEW YEAR EXHIBITION: CHIL-DREN IN CHINESE ART
January 26–March 2, 1991
Organized under the auspices of the China Institute Women's Association

58. ANCIENT CHINESE BRONZE ART: CAST-ING THE PRECIOUS SACRAL VESSEL
April 20–June 15, 1991
Curator: W. Thomas Chase

59. EARLY CHINESE CERAMICS FROM NEW YORK STATE MUSEUMS
October 19–December 14, 1991
Curator: Martie W. Young

60. TREASURES OF THE LAST EMPEROR: SELECTIONS FROM THE PALACE MUSEUM, BEIJING
February 1–March 7, 1992
Curator: Lawrence Wu

61. LAMAS, PRINCES AND BRIGANDS: PHO-TOGRAPHS BY JOSEPH ROCK OF THE TIBETAN BORDERLANDS OF CHINA
April 15–July 31, 1992
Curator: Michael Aris

*62. WORD AS IMAGE: THE ART OF CHI-NESE SEAL ENGRAVING
October 21–December 12, 1992
Curator: Jason C. Kuo

63. A YEAR OF GOOD FORTUNE–1993: LEG-ENDS OF THE ROOSTER AND TRADI-TIONS OF THE CHINESE NEW YEAR
January 19–March 6, 1993
Curator: Willow Weilan Hai

64. DISCARDING THE BRUSH: GAO QIPEI, 1660-1734
April 17–June 12, 1993
Curator: Klass Ruitenbeek
Organized by the Rijksmuseum Amsterdam

65. AS YOU WISH: SYMBOL AND MEANING ON CHINESE PORCELAINS FROM THE TAFT MUSEUM
October 23–January 15, 1994
Curator: David T. Johnson

66. SENDING AWAY THE OLD, WELCOMING THE NEW
February 5–March 5, 1994
Curator: Karen Kane

67. CAPTURING A WORLD: CHINA AND ITS PEOPLE—PHOTOGRAPHY BY JOHN THOMSON
March 26–June 11, 1994
Organized by the British Council; catalogue by the British Council

68. AT THE DRAGON COURT: CHINESE EMBROIDERED MANDARIN SQUARES FROM THE SCHUYLER V.R. CAMMANN COLLECTION
October 20–December 22, 1994
Brochure from similar show which took place at Yale Univ. Art Gallery
Curator: John Finlay

69. ANIMALS OF THE CHINESE ZODIAC: CELEBRATING CHINESE NEW YEAR
January 20–March 4, 1995
Curator: Willow Weilan Hai

*70. CHINESE PORCELAINS OF THE SEVEN-TEENTH CENTURY: LANDSCAPES, SCHOLARS' MOTIFS AND NARRATIVES
April 22–August 5, 1995
Curator: Julia B. Curtis

71. ABSTRACTION AND EXPRESSION IN CHINESE CALLIGRAPHY
October 14–December 21, 1995
Curator: H. Christopher Luce
(Exhibition traveled to the Seattle Art Museum, Seattle, Washington, November 21, 1996 to March 23, 1997 and to the Santa Barbara Museum of Art, Santa Bar-bara, California,
September 18, 1999 to November 21, 1999.)

72. CALLIGRAPHY AS LIVING ART: SELEC-TIONS FROM THE JILL SACKLER CHI-NESE
CALLIGRAPHY COMPETITION
February 3–March 9, 1996
Curator: Willow Weilan Hai, in conjunc-tion with the A. M. Sackler Foundation, Washington, D.C.

73. HARE'S FUR, TORTOISESHELL AND PARTRIDGE FEATHERS CHINESE BROWN- AND BLACK-GLAZED CERAMICS, 400-1400
April 20–July 6, 1996
Curator: Robert Mowry
Organized by the Harvard University Art Museum, Massachusetts

*74. THE LIFE OF A PATRON: ZHOU LIANG-GONG (1612-1672) AND THE PAINTERS OF SEVENTEENTH-CENTURY CHINA
October 23–December 21, 1996
Curator: Hongnam Kim

75. ADORNMENT FOR ETERNITY: STATUS AND RANK IN CHINESE ORNAMENT
February 6–July 14, 1997
Curators: Julia White and Emma Bunker
Organized by the Denver Art Museum

*76. POWER AND VIRTUE: THE HORSE IN CHINESE ART
September 11–December 13, 1997
Curator: Robert E. Harrist, Jr.

77. SCENT OF INK: THE ROY AND MARILYN PAPP COLLECTION OF CHINESE ART
February 5–June 20, 1998
Curator: Claudia Brown
Organized by the Phoenix Art Museum

78. CHINESE SNUFF BOTTLES FROM THE PAMELA R. LESSING FRIEDMAN COLLECTION
September 16–December 13, 1998
Organized by the Asian Art Coordinating Council

*79. A LITERATI LIFE IN THE TWENTIETH CENTURY: WANG FANGYU—ARTIST, SCHOLAR, CONNOISSEUR
February 11–June 20, 1999
Curator: H. Christopher Luce

*80. THE RESONANCE OF THE QIN IN EAST ASIAN ART
September 16–December 12, 1999
Curator: Stephen Addiss

81. 2000 NEW YEAR EXHIBITION: THE STORY OF RED
January 12–February 11, 2000
Curator: Willow Weilan Hai Chang

*82. DAWN OF THE YELLOW EARTH: ANCIENT CHINESE CERAMICS FROM THE MEIYINTANG COLLECTION
March 21–June 18, 2000
Curator: Regina Krahl
(Exhibition traveled to the Fresno Metropolitan Museum of Art, Fresno, California, August 11, 2000 to November 12, 2000.)

* 83. THE CHINESE PAINTER AS POET
September 14–December 10, 2000
Curator: Jonathan Chaves

84. LIVING HERITAGE: VERNACULAR ENVIRONMENT IN CHINA
January 25–June 10, 2001
Curator: Kai-yin Lo

*85. EXQUISITE MOMENTS: WEST LAKE & SOUTHERN SONG ART
September 25–December 9, 2001
Curator: Hui-shu Lee

86. CIRCLES OF REFLECTION: THE CARTER COLLECTION OF CHINESE BRONZE MIRRORS
February 7–June 2, 2002
Curator: Ju-hsi Chou

*87. BLANC DE CHINE: DIVINE IMAGES IN PORCELAIN
September 19–December 7, 2002
Curator: John Ayer

88. WEAVING CHINA'S PAST: THE AMY S. CLAGUE COLLECTION OF CHINESE TEXTILES
January 29–June 7, 2003
Curator: Claudia Brown

*89. PASSION FOR THE MOUNTAINS: 17TH CENTURY LANDSCAPE PAINTINGS FROM THE NANJING MUSEUM
September 18–December 20, 2003
Curator: Willow Weilan Hai Chang

90. GOLD & JADE: IMPERIAL JEWELRY OF THE MING DYNASTY FROM THE NANJING MUNICIPAL MUSEUM
February 12–June 5, 2004
Organized by Nanjing Municipal Museum & the China Institute Gallery

91. THE SCHOLAR AS COLLECTOR: CHINESE ART AT YALE
September 23–December 11, 2004
Curator: David Ake Sensabaugh

*92. PROVIDING FOR THE AFTERLIFE: "BRILLIANT ARTIFACTS" FROM SHANDONG
February 3–June 4, 2005
Curators: Susan L. Beningson & Carry Liu

93. MASTERPIECES OF CHINESE LACQUER FROM THE MIKE HEALY COLLECTION
September 16–December 3, 2005
Curator: Julia M. White
Organized by the Honolulu Academy of Arts

*94. TRADE TASTE & TRANSFORMATION: JINGDEZHEN PORCELAIN FOR JAPAN, 1620–1645
February 2–June 10, 2006
Curator: Julia B. Curtis
(Exhibition traveled to the Honolulu Academy of Arts, Hawaii, July 19–October 8, 2006.)

95. THE BEAUTY OF CHINESE GARDENS
June 28–August 12, 2006
Organized by the China Institute Gallery

*96. SHU: REINVENTING BOOKS IN CONTEMPORARY CHINESE ART
Part I: September 28–November 11, 2006
Part II: December 13–February 24, 2007
Curator: Wu Hung
(Exhibition traveled to Seattle Asian Art Museum, Washington, August 9–December 2, 2007 and Honolulu Academy of Arts, Hawaii, June 25–August 31, 2008.)

97. TEA, WINE AND POETRY: THE ART OF DRINKING VESSELS THE INTERNATIONAL ASIAN ART FAIR, NEW YORK
March 23–March 28, 2007
Organized by the China Institute Gallery

98. TEA, WINE AND POETRY: QING DYNASTY LITERATI AND THEIR DRINKING VESSELS
March 24–June 16, 2007
Curators: Guo Ruoyu and Soong Shu Kong
Organized by the University Museum and Art Gallery, The University of Hong Kong

*99. BUDDHIST SCULPTURE FROM CHINA: SELECTIONS FROM XI'AN BEILIN MUSEUM, FIFTH THROUGH NINTH CENTURIES
September 20–December 8, 2007
Curator: Annette L. Juliano

*100. ENCHANTED STORIES: CHINESE SHADOW THEATER IN SHAANXI
January 31–May 11, 2008
Curators: Chen Shanqiao, Li Hongjun, and Zhao Nong
Organized by China Institute Gallery in collaboration with Shaanxi Provincial Art Gallery

101. BEIJING 2008: A PHOTOGRAPHIC JOURNEY
June 12–August 17, 2008
A special exhibition organized by the China Institute Gallery and the Beijing Archive Bureau

*102. THE LAST EMPEROR'S COLLECTION: MASTERPIECES OF PAINTING AND CALLIGRAPHY FROM THE LIAONING PROVINCIAL MUSEUM
September 25–December 14, 2008
Curators: Willow Weilan Hai Chang, Yang Renkai, and David Ake Sensabaugh

103. NOBLE TOMBS AT MAWANGDUI: ART AND LIFE IN THE CHANGSHA KINGDOM, THIRD CENTURY BCE TO FIRST CENTURY CE
February 12–June 7, 2009
Curator: Chen Jianming
Organized by China Institute Gallery and Hunan Provincial Museum
(Exhibition traveled to Santa Barbara Museum of Art, September 19–December 13, 2009.)

*104. HUMANISM IN CHINA: A CONTEMPORARY RECORD OF PHOTOGRAPHY
September 24 – December 13, 2009
Organized by the Guangdong Museum of Art.
Re-organized by China Institute Gallery and Jerome Silbergeld.

* Exhibition catalogues currently available for sale.
For information on the availability of these titles and others,
please contact China Institute in America at (212) 744-8181.

China Institute

116

Helen Y. and William E. Little
Robert W. and Virginia Riggs Lyons
Clare Tweedy McMorris & Howard McMorris, III
Gerard M. Meistrell
William N. Raiford
Howard and Mary Ann Rogers
Robert Rosenkranz and Alexandra Munroe
Diane H. Schafer and Jeffrey A. Stein
Mei Wu Stanton
Martha Sutherland and Barnaby Conrad III
Ann Tanenbaum
Charles J. Tanenbaum
Patricia P. Tang
Theow H. Tow
Shao Fang and Cheryl L. Wang
Laura B. Whitman and Thomas Danziger
Yvonne L. C. and Frederick Wong
Denis C. and Kathleen Yang
Evelyn B. Younes

GALLERY COMMITTEE

Diane H. Schafer, *Chair*
Agnes Gund, *Vice-Chair*
Yvonne L.C. Wong, *Vice-Chair*

Susan L. Beningson
Claudia Brown
John R. Curtis, Jr.
Mary Wadsworth Darby
Jane DeBevoise
Robert E. Harrist, Jr.
Maxwell K. Hearn
Annette L. Juliano
Virgina A. Kamsky
David Ake Sensabaugh
Jerome Silbergeld
Sophia Sheng
Nancy S. Steinhardt
Marie-Hélène Weill
I. Peter Wolff

GALLERY STAFF

Willow Weilan Hai Chang, *Director*
Sara Tam, *Registrar and Manager*
Mia Myoungsook Park, *Coordinator*
Yue Ma, *Assistant*

DOCENTS

Elisa Chen
Viviane Chen
Lillia Chrysostome
Roberta Nitka
Patricia Reilly
Betty Tom
Xin Wang

VOLUNTEERS

Ann Dillon
Jackie Handel
Margaret Ma
Lynn Ohrenstein
Gloria Young